DATE DUE

**UNDERSTANDING   AND
MANAGING   LEARNING
DISABILITIES   IN   ADULTS**
Dale R. Jordan
Book

UNDERSTANDING AND MANAGING LEARNING DISABILITIES IN ADULTS

The Professional Practices in Adult Education and Human Resource Development Series explores issues and concerns of practitioners who work in the broad range of settings in adult and continuing education and human resource development.

The books are intended to provide information and strategies on how to make practice more effective for professionals and those they serve. They are written from a practical viewpoint and provide a forum for instructors, administrators, policy makers, counselors, trainers, managers, program and organizational developers, instructional designers, and other related professionals.

Editorial correspondence should be sent to the Editor-in-Chief:

Michael W. Galbraith
Professional Practices Series
Krieger Publishing Company
P.O. Box 9542
Melbourne, FL 32902-9542

UNDERSTANDING AND MANAGING LEARNING DISABILITIES IN ADULTS

Dale R. Jordan, Ph.D.

KRIEGER PUBLISHING COMPANY
MALABAR, FLORIDA
2000

Original Edition   2000

Printed and Published by
KRIEGER PUBLISHING COMPANY
KRIEGER DRIVE
MALABAR, FLORIDA 32950

Copyright © 2000 by Dale R. Jordan

Library of Congress Cataloging-In-Publication Data

Jordan, Dale R.
    Understanding and managing learning disabilities in adults / Dale R. Jordan. — Original ed.
        p.   cm. — (The professional practices in adult education and human resource development series)
    Includes bibliographical references (p.   ) and index.
    ISBN 1-57524-108-0 (cloth : alk. paper)
    1. Learning disabled—Education—United States.   2. Learning disabilities—United States.   I. Title.   II. Series.
    LC4818.5.J672   2000
    371.92'6—dc21   99-26327
                                                             CIP

10   9   8   7   6   5   4   3   2

To my sister Ila Bell, who has been
a major source of inspiration all my life.
Her quiet spiritual strength has helped our family
overcome incredible challenges
from threatening emotional shadows
that are described in these pages.

CONTENTS

PREFACE

A cheerful heart is good medicine.
But a crushed spirit dries up the bones.
Proverbs 17:22 (New International Version)

For more than 40 years I have been immersed in the challenge of changing crushed spirits into cheerful hearts in countless adults who struggle with learning disabilities (LD). The good medicine of a cheerful heart finally comes to LD adults when hope replaces despair. This healing of emotions and feelings does not start with instruction in reading skills or workplace competency. Instead, crushed spirits begin to revive as LD individuals learn the truth about themselves. "Why have I always struggled so hard with school learning? Am I too 'dumb' to do what my family and friends learn easily? Why do I feel so sad and depressed? Why am I afraid of so many things? Why can't I pay attention? Why am I so disorganized? Why do I have a quick temper that gets me into trouble? Why can't I hold a job? Why am I so worthless? Why can't I stay in love and make a good life? Why can't I get rid of old guilt and shame?"

As answers come to these lifelong questions, LD adults experience a profound inner healing that replaces despair with hope. Spirits that were crushed by chronic failure spring up on wings of new self-understanding: "You mean I'm not dumb? All my life I've thought I was stupid. You mean I'm LD, but I'm not stupid?" From this starting point of new joy, LD adults thrive and develop for the first time in their lives.

This book is about replacing crushed spirits with cheerful hearts. In simple language, each chapter answers questions never before answered for thousands of LD adults. Chapter 1 explains several types of specific learning disabilities that make classroom performance difficult for 15% of the general population. Included are practical strategies for managing these forms of learning disability. Chapter 2 presents new information about how the higher brain, midbrain, and brain stem work together in processing new information and building long-term memory. This chapter explains how differences in brain pathway development cause LD. Chapter 3 explores the many faces of Nonverbal LD (NVLD) in adults. It describes awkward social behaviors that are linked to very high functioning autism in adults. Chapter 3 ends with management strategies for reducing conflict in Asperger's syndrome and other types of NVLD, which are commonly seen when bright adults fail to build successful lives. Chapter 4 presents in-depth information about Social-Emotional LD (SELD) that disrupts society in destructive ways. This chapter explains the role of the limbic system (midbrain) in controlling antisocial emotions that often accompany LD in adults. Chapter 4 concludes with management strategies, including medications that greatly reduce the social impact of SELD. Chapter 5 describes the wide range of disabling emotions and feelings that often exist in the shadows of LD. It explains types of depression and mania, as well as the link between LD and anxiety. Management strategies are given for reducing depression, manic behaviors, and chronic anxiety in LD adults. Chapter 6 presents new insights into the impact of learning disabilities as adults age. This chapter shows important differences between types of dimentia, severe depression, and LD in aging adults. Strategies are presented for managing learning disabilities in the aging population. Chapter 7 discusses what lies ahead in understanding and managing LD in adults. This chapter reviews promising techniques in diagnosing and managing LD.

The information presented in this book will set free many spirits who have been crushed by lifelong LD. The goal of this book is to bring the good medicine of a cheerful heart to LD adults as they encounter the challenges of the new century.

THE AUTHOR

In 1957, Dale Jordan began his career as an elementary classroom teacher with youngsters who could not read, write, or spell without a great deal of help. In those days little was known about dyslexia, attention deficit disorders, Nonverbal LD, Social-Emotional LD, or disruptive emotions that hide in the shadows of learning disabilities. After several years of mainstream classroom teaching without specialized help for struggling learners, Jordan entered a Ph.D. program in educational psychology and reading education to find answers to the burning question: "Why can't these bright individuals learn to read, write, and spell?" To his surprise, no answers were forthcoming through university courses of that day. Jordan's doctoral committee at the University of Oklahoma permitted him to develop a field-based research plan that enabled him to evaluate adults within prison systems, military units, the workplace, and mental health institutions. That research revealed the astonishing prevalence of what came to be called learning disabilities (LD) in adults in every walk of life.

From that experience, Jordan began to define dyslexia and how this type of LD impacts personal life, classroom performance, and workplace success. In 1968 he inaugurated a university training program to prepare classroom teachers to recognize dyslexia and to modify classroom strategies to meet the special needs of LD students. In 1972 Jordan published the landmark study *Dyslexia in the Classroom,* one of the first discussions of LD in lifelong learning. After several years in university teaching, Jordan and his wife established a private practice for diagnosing and remediating all types of LD in children, adolescents, and adults. Through one-on-one interaction with struggling learners from around the world, the Jordan Diagnostic Center in Oklahoma City continued to research learning disabilities and their impact on countless lives.

Jordan has authored 27 books and curriculum programs for LD learners. For 30 years he has been a prolific workshop presenter and seminar leader with workplace leaders, corrections officials, mental health providers, the judiciary, vocational rehabilitation counselors, and other agencies that confront LD in adults. Through this international outreach, Jordan has taught three generations of educators how to replace crushed spirits in LD adults with the good medicine of a cheerful heart.

CHAPTER 1

What Is Learning Disability in Adults?

HISTORY OF LEARNING DISABILITY

The struggle to learn that now is called *learning disability* (LD) was first described in the 1880s by two German physicians, Reinhold Berlin and Ludwig Lichteim. They were bewildered by the fact that certain intelligent persons could not learn to read, regardless of how they were taught. Berlin was the first to use the word *dyslexia* to describe poor reading in otherwise bright individuals (Berlin, 1884). Lichteim introduced the word *alexia* to describe total inability to learn to read (Lichteim, 1885). Soon the term *word blindness* was added to these studies of poor readers (Berlin, 1887). Word blindness described a type of reading disability often seen with dyslexia. Persons with normal visual acuity (20/20 or 20/30) could not "see" black print on white paper, especially under bright light. Printed patterns twisted, swirled, moved around the page, and became so distorted that reading was impossible.

At the same time, the American psychologist William James described another type of learning problem that involved hyperactivity, mood swings, impulsivity, rebellion against rules, and disruptive behavior (James, 1890). At the turn of the century, the British physician George Still expanded upon James's work by defining problems in paying attention (Still, 1902). A few years later, Alfred Tredgold made the first connection between brain structure and disruptive, inattentive behavior (Tredgold, 1908). He demonstrated that certain kinds of medication reduced hyperactivity and increased attention span in disruptive learners.

Research into the causes of dyslexia, alexia, and word blindness began in the United States following World War I. In the 1920s, the American neurologist Samuel T. Orton studied what he named *strephosymbolia,* or "twisted symbols," in adults who had suffered left brain injuries (Orton, 1925). It was not until 1962 that Samuel Kirk introduced the concept and label *learning disability* (Kirk, 1962). Kirk believed that brain structure was somehow responsible for differences in learning ability. He speculated that certain individuals struggle to learn because of brain-based "disability" caused by differences in how brain pathways are formed.

WHAT IS LEARNING DISABILITY?

During the 1960s and 1970s, national and international organizations tried to develop a standard definition of LD that would guide everyone in dealing with struggling learners. However, it has not yet been possible to achieve a single definition of LD. Kirk's original proposal remains a reliable description of LD:

> A learning disability refers to a retardation, disorder, or delayed development in one or more of the processes of speech, language, reading, writing, arithmetic, or other school subjects resulting from a psychological handicap caused by a possible cerebral dysfunction and/or emotional or behavioral disturbances. It is not the result of mental retardation, sensory deprivation, or cultural and instructional factors. (Kirk, 1962, p. 263)

LEARNING DISABILITY IN ADULTHOOD

Before 1985 most definitions of LD were addressed to childhood problems in learning. During the 1980s the U.S. Office of Special Education and Rehabilitation Services made the first official attempt to define LD in the workplace (RSA, 1985). In 1993 Henry Reiff, Paul Gerber, and Rick Ginsberg presented a composite definition of LD in adults that incorporated main issues from other definitions:

> Learning disabilities in adulthood affect each individual uniquely. For some, difficulties lie in only one specific functional area; for others, problems are more global in nature, including social and emotional problems. For many, certain functional areas of adult life are limited compared to other areas. Adults with learning disabilities are of average or above-

average intelligence, but intelligence oftentimes has no relation to the degree of disability. Learning disabilities persist throughout the lifespan, with some areas improving and others worsening. Although specific deficits associated with learning disabilities are real and persistent, such deficits do not necessarily preclude achievement and, in some cases, may have a positive relationship with achievement. In almost all cases, learning disabilities necessitate alternative approaches to achieve vocational and personal success. (Reiff et al., pp. 19–20)

TYPES OF LD IN ADULTS

It is unusual for a person with learning disability to have only one type of LD. Most individuals who struggle to learn have several forms of learning difficulty, much like layers of an onion. This overlapping of learning problems is called *comorbidity*. Before struggling learners can be taught successfully, each layer of difficulty must be recognized. As research into the nature of LD continued into the 1990s, it became clear that the label "learning disability" was too ambiguous to be helpful to instructors. By 1990 the label LD had gained four distinct meanings (Jordan, 1996a, 1996b). *First,* LD can refer to specific learning disabilities, such as dyslexia, dysgraphia, dyscalculia, or attention deficit disorders. *Second,* LD can refer to learning difference, such as dominant brain modalities that cause individuals to be visual learners, auditory learners, or tactile/kinesthetic learners. *Third,* LD can refer to learning difficulty, such as very slow perceptual speed (slow rate of processing), or Scotopic Sensitivity syndrome. *Fourth,* LD can refer to late development, often called "late bloomer." Saying that a person is LD is inadequate to explain his or her struggle to learn.

DYSLEXIA

Dyslexia was the first type of specific learning disability to be described (Berlin, 1884). A century after Berlin's pioneering research, I presented a comprehensive definition of dyslexia in adults:

Dyslexia is the inability of an intelligent person to become fluent in the basic skills of reading, spelling, and handwriting in spite of prolonged teaching and tutoring. Math computation may also remain at the level of struggle. Dyslexia means that the person will always struggle to some degree with reading printed passages, writing with a pen or pencil, spelling accurately from memory, and developing sentences and paragraphs with correct grammar and punctuation. Dyslexia may also include difficulty telling oral information accurately. No matter how hard the person tries, certain types of errors continue to appear in reading, writing, and spelling. Dyslexia is a brain-based dysfunction that often is genetic. It tends to run in families. Through certain kinds of remedial training, dyslexic patterns can be partly overcome or reduced, but dyslexia cannot be completely eliminated. It is a lifelong, brain-based condition that most dyslexics can learn to compensate for successfully. (Jordan, 1989a, p. 8)

Types of Dyslexia

During the 1980s the National Institutes of Health and other research agencies agreed to designate the 1990s as the "Decade of the Brain." A major emphasis would be placed upon discovering as much as possible about brain functions in learning. During this Decade of the Brain, Sally Shaywitz, a neurologist at Yale University School of Medicine, developed a brain map that shows how the left brain normally handles the reading process (Shaywitz, 1996). Using a new generation of brain imaging technology called functional magnetic resonant imaging (fMRI), Shaywitz tracked the eight-step sequence the left brain uses for reading (see Figure 1.1). In most persons, these "reading pathways" developed steadily as the brain matures during childhood and adolescence. Dyslexia is caused when too many "bridges" are out along the "reading pathways" shown in the Shaywitz model.

Visual Dyslexia

Three decades of neurological research have revealed that dyslexia is caused by many differences in nerve pathway development throughout the left brain (Galaburda, 1983; Geschwind, 1984; Jordan, 1989a, 1989b, 1996a, 1998; Shaywitz, 1996). Sometimes portions of the right brain also are involved. Most persons who are dyslexic have trouble interpreting what they see in print. Certain letters and numerals tend to reverse or turn upside down (b–d p–q n–u m–w b–p f–t 3–E 7–L 6–9 2–5). Inside parts of words

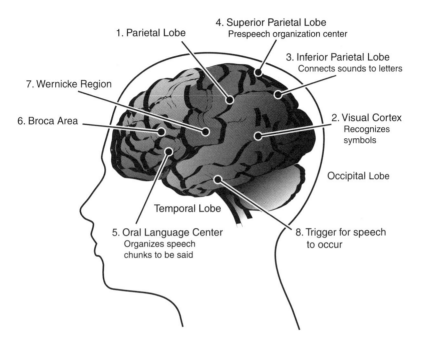

Figure 1.1. Shaywitz has shown the eight-step circuit in the left brain where normal reading occurs. *Step 1.* The parietal lobe receives new visual information related to reading. *Step 2.* This visual data is fired to the visual cortex where symbols are recognized and organized. *Step 3.* This organized visual data is sent to the inferior parietal lobe where sounds connect to letters. *Step 4.* The sound/letter blends are fired to the superior parietal lobe where speech patterns are preorganized. *Step 5.* This sound/letter data is now fired to the oral language center in the temporal lobe. *Step 6.* The broca area further organizes the speech material. *Step 7.* This refined speech material is then fired to the Wernicke region which puts the final touches on what is about to be spoken. *Step 8.* If the person is reading aloud, the speech organs are triggered to say what the eyes have seen on the page. If the person is reading silently, *Step 8* translates the reading data into "brain language" that lets the frontal lobe and prefrontal cortex know what the eyes have seen.

tend to reverse (Apirl–April bran–barn from–form). Dyslexic readers scramble syllables, which causes them to misinterpret what they see (Tulsa/Altus reserve/reverse butter/tubber). This problem with interpreting what one sees is called *visual dyslexia* because the visual cortex of the left brain does not learn how to recognize printed symbols in the right direction and sequence. Figure 1.2 shows how visual dyslexia interferes with reading and word recognition. These dyslexic reversals and scrambles occur without warning. Readers who are dyslexic never know when they will get things backward, upside down, or out of sequence.

Auditory Dyslexia

Along with scrambling and reversing of visual symbols, we usually find another form of dyslexia that keeps individuals from hearing softer/slower speech sounds. Often this is called "tone deafness" because the person does not hear separate sounds of speech (phonemes) that are spoken slowly and softly. Early in the Decade of the Brain, Paula Tallal at Rutgers University reported the main cause for tone deafness, or auditory dyslexia (Tallal et al. 1993). Part of the midbrain, the medial geniculate nucleus, is designed to recognize and organize the hard/fast, soft/slow speech sounds we hear and say (see Figure 1.3). In persons who are not dyslexic, the medial geniculate nucleus processes speech sounds at the speed of 40 milliseconds or faster. When dyslexia exists, the midbrain is considerably slower in sorting out and organizing the sounds of speech. Individuals with this midbrain deficit cannot learn phonics by hearing it. They cannot develop long-term memory for accurate spelling. They continually misunderstand what others say. As they listen to instructions and conversations, again and again they ask "What?" or "Huh?" or "What do you mean?" Figure 1.4 shows how tone deafness appears on paper. No matter how hard the person with auditory dyslexia tries, he or she ends up spelling like the examples in Figure 1.4.

Dysgraphia

Most persons who are dyslexic never learn to do good handwriting. Regardless of how much they practice writing, they can-

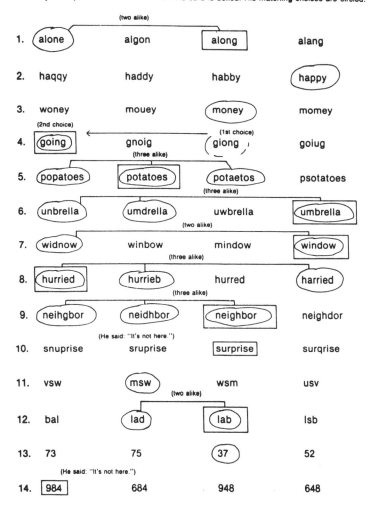

Visual Memory—The pattern the student saw on the card is boxed. His matching choices are circled.

Figure 1.2. For each line, this 37-year-old man saw a pattern on a card. He spelled each one aloud, then tried to find the same pattern on the page. As his eyes refocused from word to word on the line, his visual cortex saw changing images. Letters reversed, scrambled out of sequence, or turned upside down. On several lines, his brain saw two or three patterns that "looked alike." This activity is from the *Slingerland Screening Tests for Identifying Children with Specific Language Disabilities: Form C.* It is shown here by permission of Educators Publishing Service, Inc.

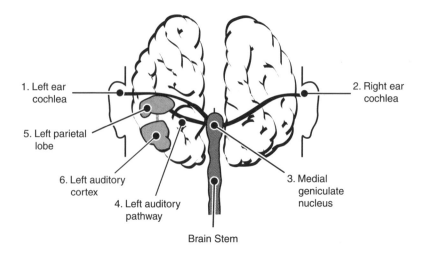

1. Left ear cochlea

2. Right ear cochlea

5. Left parietal lobe

6. Left auditory cortex

3. Medial geniculate nucleus

4. Left auditory pathway

Brain Stem

Figure 1.3. The Tallal model shows how the left brain interprets oral language. First, the cochlea structures of each ear (1 and 2) gather sound energy and send it to the *medial geniculate nucleus* (3) in the midbrain. Second, the medial geniculate nucleus separates the speech sounds (phonemes) into bundles of hard/fast and soft/slow chunks. These speech bundles then are organized in the correct sequence. Third, pairs of specialized cells along the *left auditory pathway* (4) transfer these bundles of hard/fast, soft/slow speech chunks to the *left parietal lobe* (5) which fires this oral information to the *left auditory cortex* (6) within the left temporal lobe. The hard/fast sound chunks arrive first, then wait while the soft/slow chunks arrive more slowly. Fourth, the left auditory cortex blends these hard/fast, soft/slow sound chunks into the oral language we speak, hear, and spell. When cell structures are partly formed within the medial geniculate nucleus, a condition called "tone deafness" exists in failing to hear speech chunks.

not master the finger control required for good penmanship. Even when they know what to write, the pencil or pen tries to turn the opposite way in making curving strokes. Dysgraphic writers can slowly draw a few words clearly, but soon fine motor coordination breaks down and handwriting becomes too messy to read. Figure 1.5 shows the region of the left brain that controls finger movements for handwriting in persons who are right handed. Nerve pathways linking the motor cortex with finger muscles deliver confused signals that cause backward strokes, irregular size

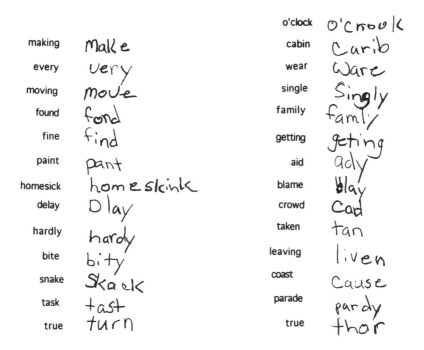

Figure 1.4. Spelling looks like this when the left auditory cortex fails to receive hard/fast, soft/slow sound chunks in the right sequence. Tone deafness to soft/slow vowels and consonants made it impossible for this 27-year-old man to build long-term memory of correct spelling patterns.

of letters, uneven spacing, and the messy appearance of dysgraphic handwriting. Figure 1.6 shows examples of dysgraphia in writing and math. No matter how hard these individuals try to write neatly, it is impossible for them to produce tidy written work.

Dyscalculia

Individuals who are dyslexic usually struggle to learn arithmetic computation and algebraic concepts. Abstract word problems make no sense, nor can these struggling learners remember the hundreds of math facts that are taught in elementary school. This part of the dyslexic maze is called *dyscalculia*. Regardless of how hard these persons try, adolescents and adults with dyscalculia cannot build long-term memory of which direction to go in

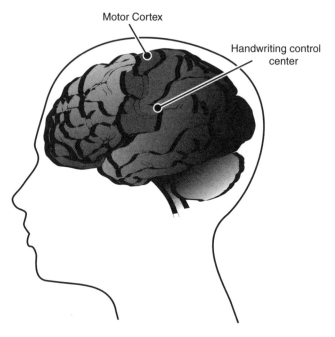

Figure 1.5. This map of the left brain shows the region of the left motor cortex that generates finger-motion signals for handwriting in right-handed persons (97%). A similar region of the right motor cortex regulates handwriting for left-handed individuals (3%). When some of the nerve pathways in the motor cortex are incompletely developed, the fingers receive confused signals that create dysgraphia.

adding, subtracting, multiplying, dividing, and working algebra equations. Figure 1.7 shows regions of the left brain and right brain where math information is processed. In working math problems, individuals with dyscalculia cannot remember whether to start on the right, on the left, at the bottom, or at the top. Figure 1.8 shows examples of math struggle in dyscalculia. Figure 1.9 shows the kind of pencil practice dyslexic persons must do on scratch paper as they search for correct answers.

How Many Persons Are Dyslexic?

Before anyone can estimate how many individuals are dyslexic, it is necessary to ask another question: How severe are

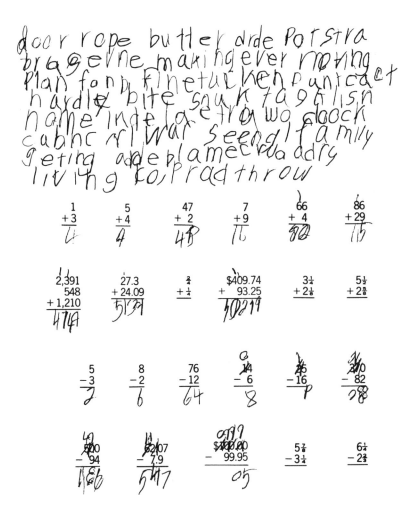

Figure 1.6. This 42-year-old man has never learned to write legibly, no matter how hard he tries. The finger-motion center of his left motor cortex sends confused signals as he spells and as he works math problems. He cannot guide the pencil to space between words or make legible strokes while writing letters. Dysgraphia often makes it impossible to read the numbers he writes in math problems.

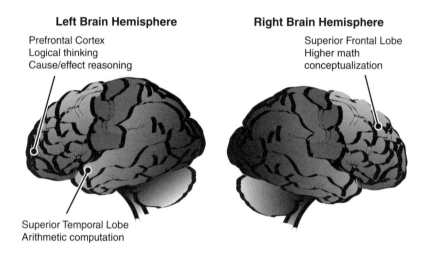

Left Brain Hemisphere

Prefrontal Cortex
Logical thinking
Cause/effect reasoning

Right Brain Hemisphere

Superior Frontal Lobe
Higher math
conceptualization

Superior Temporal Lobe
Arithmetic computation

Figure 1.7. These regions of the left brain and right brain are involved in arithmetic computation, solving problems of logic and cause/effect relationships, and higher math conceptualization.

dyslexic symptoms? In diagnosing dyslexia, we use a scale that shows levels of severity:

1	2	3		4	5	6	7		8	9	10
	mild				moderate					severe	

Most researchers agree that 5% of the general population are at the severe level of dyslexic symptoms. This is called *deep dyslexia,* or primary dyslexia (Jordan, 1996a, 1996b, 1998). This severe form of dyslexia does not decline as individuals grow older. Reading always is a struggle and remains stuck below fourth grade level. Spelling and writing seldom grow above fourth grade level. Deep dyslexia runs down family lines. It is carried by Chromosomes 6 and 15 in the DNA chain. So many nerve pathways in the left brain are underdeveloped, it is impossible for those with deep dyslexia to become fully literate. Yet persons with deep dyslexia are bright, often far above average in intelligence.

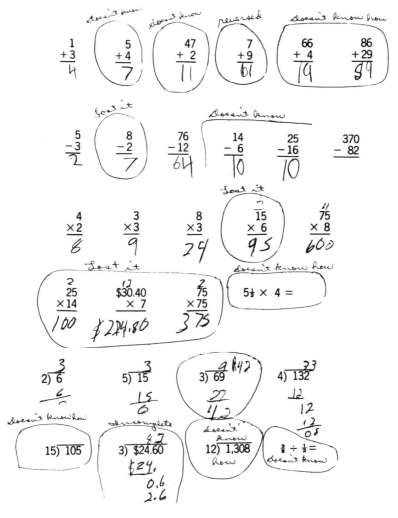

Figure 1.8. This 29-year-old woman has dyscalculia. She has never been able to learn arithmetic computation. She attended school 13 years, including kindergarten. No matter how hard she tries, she cannot build long-term memory for arithmetic information. With a hand calculator, she can work math problems correctly.

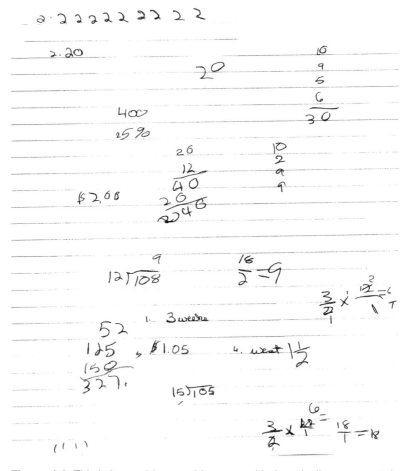

Figure 1.9. This is how a 32-year-old woman with dyscalculia uses scratch paper to search for correct answers in math assignments. Her memory for math facts is too loose and unorganized to let her find answers without combining several sensory pathways. She must see it/say it/hear it/write it simultaneously before math facts come together. Her only way to work math problems successfully is to use a hand calculator.

Another 10% in our culture are at the moderate level of severity. This is called *developmental dyslexia,* or secondary dyslexia (Jordan, 1996a, 1996b, 1998). This moderate form of dyslexia partly fades away as the individual matures during adolescence and early adulthood. Such a person might have been at Level 8 in severity during childhood. By age 14, he or she might be down to Level 6 in severity. By age 17, dyslexic symptoms might be down to Level 5. By age 25, dyslexia might be down to Level 4 or lower, allowing the person to succeed in college or even in graduate school.

SCOTOPIC SENSITIVITY SYNDROME

In 1887 Lichteim and Berlin began to study a puzzling reading disability they named *word blindness.* Individuals who had good outdoor vision (20/20 acuity) could not see to read. When they looked at black print on white paper, they did not see clearly printed letters and words in lines. Instead, they saw moving, twisting print distortions like those shown in Figure 1.10. These distorted visual images move sideways, up and down, swirl like a turning wheel, spread apart, and become so blurred that letters and words disappear into black smudges. Portions of words flicker, or fade away, then come back. In 1976 Helen Irlen at Long Beach Community College discovered that placing color on the page stopped these print distortions for some individuals. Irlen called this *Scotopic Sensitivity Syndrome* (SSS). By 1990, Irlen had developed a highly structured diagnostic procedure to find the right color or combination of colors for persons who suffer from Scotopic Sensitivity (Irlen, 1991).

A full century after Berlin and Lichteim first described word blindness, three research teams mapped the brain dysfunctions that cause this type of LD. Margaret Livingstone at Harvard School of Medicine identified incompletely developed cells along the magnicellular pathway that links the retina of each eye with the anterior geniculate nucleus in the midbrain (Livingstone et al., 1991). For the first time, we had a scientific explanation of why many intelligent, often dyslexic individuals cannot "see" to read. Livingstone's research gained support when Stephen Lehmkuhle at the University of Missouri replicated the Harvard studies of the magnicellular

Luis squeezed Maria's hand as they felt the airplane dip downward for the last time. Together they held their breath waiting for the squeal of tires against the runway. Suddenly they felt the landing bump. Then the engines roared with a mighty backward push. The airplane slowed its race down the runway. Through their tears of joy Luis and Maria heard the voice of the cabin attendant saying: "Welcome to Dallas/Fort Worth. Please remain seated until the aircraft has come to a complete stop at the terminal. Have a good day in the Dallas area, or wherever your travel may take you."

Swirl Effect   As the eyes focus on a particular word, lines begin to swirl like a rotating wheel

Luis squeezed Maria's hand as they felt the airplane dip downward for the last time. Together they held their breath waiting for the squeal of tires against the runway. Suddenly they felt the landing bump. Then the engines roared with a mighty backward push. The airplane slowed its race down the runway. Through their tears of joy Luis and Maria heard the voice of the cabin attendant saying: "Welcome to Dallas/Fort Worth. Please remain seated until the aircraft has come to a complete stop at the terminal. Have a good day in the Dallas area, or wherever your travel may take you."

Smudge Effect   Letters and words move sideways and stack on top of each other, then move apart. The page is filled with moving black smudges that are impossible to read.

Luis squeezed Maria's hand as they felt the airplane dip downward for the last time. Through their tears of joy Luis and Maria heard the voice of the cabin attendant saying: "Welcome to Dallas/Fort Worth. Please remain seated until the aircraft has come to a complete stop at the terminal. Have a good day in the Dallas area, or wherever your travel may take you."

Fade Out Effect   Inside portions of words begin to fade in and out in a pulsing rhythm.

Luis squeezed   Maria'shandasthey   felttheairplanedip
downwardfor   thelasttime.Together theyheldtheir
breathwait   ingforthesqueal of tir esagainstthe   runw
Suddenlythey   felttthelandingbump.   Thentheengi   nes
roaredwithamig   htybackward push.   Theairplaneslow
itsracedowntherun   way.Throughthe   irtearsofjoy   Luis
andMariaheard   thevoiceofthecabin   attendantsaying
"WelcometoDal   las/Fort Worth.Plea   seremainseated
untiltheaircr   afthascometoacom   pletestopatthe   ga
Haveagood   dayintheDallasarea,or   whereveryour   trav
maytake   you."

Moving Rivers Effect   Words slide sideways, opening rivers of moving space that cascade up and down the page.

Figure 1.10. Persons who have Scotopic Sensitivity syndrome see these kinds of moving distortions as they try to read.

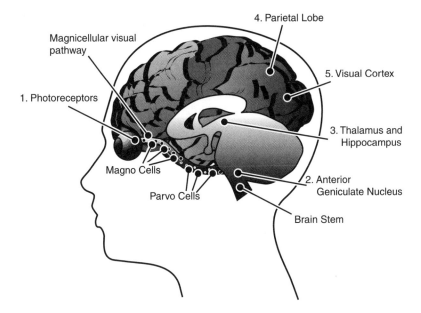

Figure 1.11. Between the retina and brain stem is the magnicellular visual pathway made of two kinds of cells that work together in pairs to carry visual impressions (1) to the midbrain. Large cells called *magno cells* quickly transfer portions of what the eyes see to the *anterior geniculate nucleus* (2). This first visual information waits while small cells called *parvo cells* more slowly deliver the rest of that visual impression. The brain stem filters out unnecessary data while the anterior geniculate nucleus starts to blend the filtered visual data into complete images. This filtered, partly organized visual information is further refined by the *thalamus* and *hippocampus* (3). Then this processed visual data is fired up to the *parietal lobes* (4). There it is classified, then fired down to the right or left *visual cortex* (5) where the brain interprets what the eyes have just seen.

Scotopic Sensitivity syndrome is caused by a double problem in nerve cell development. Portions of the magno cells are missing, like a bite out of a cookie. Also, some neurons within the anterior geniculate nucleus are incomplete. This double cellular deficit sends a cascade of unstable visual images up the chain of the brain transfers. Finally the visual cortex "sees" the print distortions shown in Figure 1.10. Adding color "fills in" the gaps in the magno cells, thus stopping the distortion cascade before it starts. Based upon research by Margaret Livingstone at Harvard Medical School, Stephen Lehmkuhle at the University of Missouri, and Guinevere Eden at the National Institute of Mental Health.

system (Lehmkuhle et al. 1993). Then Guinevere Eden at the National Institute of Mental Health reported that a portion of the magnocellular pathway (called V5) functions abnormally in dyslexic readers (Eden, 1996). Figure 1.11 shows the brain pathways where Scotopic Sensitivity syndrome (SSS) occurs. Normally, the larger magno cells transfer visual information related to motion. The smaller parvo cells transfer visual data related to shapes and colors. As research has continued into the problems related to SSS, it has become clear that this reading disorder exists to some degree in approximately 30% in the general population. Scotopic Sensitivity is found in 60% of those adults who score below fourth grade reading level. Scotopic Sensitivity is a major barrier to reading for 80% of individuals who are dyslexic (Jordan, 1996a, 1996b, 1998).

Checklist of Scotopic Sensitivity Symptoms

1. Eyes sting and burn under bright light.
2. Eyes become sleepy and want to close after reading awhile.
3. Person begins to yawn heavily while reading or copying.
4. Eyes skip words during reading or copying.
5. Eyes move down too far and skip lines while reading or copying.
6. Eyes quit looking at the page, chalkboard, or screen.
7. Person's mind starts to wander instead of concentrating.
8. Person prefers to read or work in low or indirect light.
9. Person shades eyes with hand, or wants to wear ball cap with the bill shading the eyes.
10. Person must run finger under each line to keep the place.
11. Person sees too much glare coming from white paper.
12. Lines on the page move up and down.
13. Words smudge together, then spread apart.
14. Things on the page blink on and off, or sparkle, or flash.
15. Inside portions of words fade away, then come back.
16. Eyes see a halo or "ghost image" around words.
17. Moving rivers run down the page as words slide sideways.
18. Edges swirl like a turning wheel while eyes focus on words.
19. Print pulses in and out of focus.
20. Lines seem to ripple up and down like a flag waving.

21. Words seem to fall off the edge of the page.
22. Person feels dizzy or sick riding in moving vehicles.
23. Person sleeps instead of looking out the window.
24. Things seem to come up toward the face, then go back down.
25. Things startle from the edge of vision as if coming rapidly toward the face.
26. Person feels dizzy, nauseated, or frightened on high places.
27. Person has trouble placing feet on escalators or stairways.
28. Person is afraid to ride in elevators on outside of buildings.
29. Person flinches back from approaching ball.
30. Person bumps furniture and hits doorways while moving around.

ATTENTION DEFICIT DISORDER

In 1890 the American psychologist William James described a disruptive lifestyle that interfered with classroom learning. Those persons seemed to be bright, but they were immature, hyperactive, often disregarded rules and regulations, listened poorly, and failed to develop good long-term memory (James, 1890). It was not until 1980 that the term *attention deficit disorder* was introduced by the American Psychiatric Association (*DSM-III*, American Psychiatric Association, 1980). That definition provided three categories of inattention: (1) *Attention deficit with hyperactivity* (ADD-H), (2) *Attention deficit without Hyperactivity* (ADD-H), and (3) *Attention deficit, residual type* (not outgrown). However, many prominent scientists insist that a person must be hyperactive before he or she can be labeled as having attention deficit disorder. This controversy over whether a nonhyperactive person can have attention deficit disorder remains unsettled as we enter the 21st century (Jordan, 1998).

Neurological research during the Decade of the Brain discovered how the brain controls attention. Figure 1.12 shows nine brain regions that work together in teams to command the whole brain to start paying attention, maintain attention, and shift to the next focus of attention. Attention deficit disorder occurs when any of these brain regions cannot do its job as part of the attention focus team.

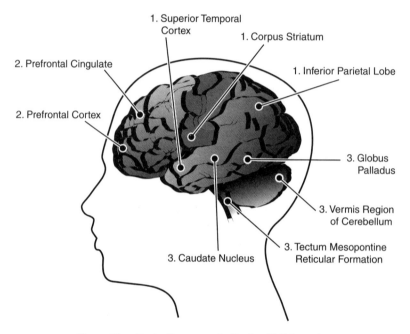

Three-Step Brain Sequence in Paying Full Attention

1. Focus Full Attention
The superior temporal cortex, corpus striatum, and inferior parietal lobe team together
to signal other brain regions to start paying attention.

2. Sustain Full Attention
The prefrontal cortex and prefrontal cingulate work together to sustain full attention
until the task is finished.

3. Shift Attention to Next Task
The caudate nucleus, globus palladus, vermis region of the cerebellum, and tectum
mesopontine reticular formation signal other brain regions to shift focus to the next
attention task.

Figure 1.12. These nine regions of the higher brain and midbrain work together as a complex team to carry out attention tasks. When any of these
links within the attention system fails to work on schedule or stops working
too soon, attention deficits occur.

The following behaviors show the presence of attention deficit disorder in adults.

ADHD-Attention Deficit Hyperactive Disorder

1. Continually fidgets and squirms
2. Cannot stay seated
3. Is too easily distracted by what goes on nearby
4. Cannot wait for his/her turn
5. Blurts out instead of waiting to speak
6. Is too quick to argue
7. Does not finish what is started
8. Cannot keep on paying attention
9. Is very quickly bored
10. Shifts from one uncompleted task to another
11. Cannot work quietly. Talks excessively. Makes too much noise
12. Interrupts. Butts in
13. Does not listen
14. Continually loses things
15. Is attracted to/thrilled by high-risk behavior
16. Automatically makes excuses. Blames others
17. Is aggressive to get his/her own way

ADD-Attention Deficit Disorder without Hyperactivity

1. Mind drifts off on mental rabbit trails
2. Has short attention span: 60 to 90 seconds at a time
3. Drifts away into private world of fantasy/make-believe
4. Comes back to attention (like waking up) off and on in cycles
5. Absorbs bits of information during "wake up" moments
6. Learned information is filled with gaps
7. Has a lifestyle that is very loose and poorly organized
8. Is absent minded. Continually forgets
9. Constantly loses things. Can't remember where they are

10. Does not finish what is started unless reminded
11. Has major tendency for depression

LD IN ADULTHOOD

These are the main types of learning disabilities that follow individuals from childhood, through adolescence, and into adulthood. Approximately 80% of LD youngsters outgrow enough of their childhood struggle to become moderately or mildly LD adults (Barkley, 1995; Jordan, 1998). The other 20% enter adulthood as severely LD as they were in childhood. It is rare to find an LD person with only one form of learning difficulty. Like layers of an onion, types of LD overlap throughout the person's lifetime. All their lives, these individuals must compensate for residual LD. In education, in the workplace, and in personal relationships, adults with LD must have understanding and a certain degree of help from others.

MANAGING LD IN ADULTS

During childhood and adolescence, parents and teachers do their best to make accommodations that enable LD youngsters to compensate for dyslexia, dysgraphia, dyscalculia, ADHD, ADD, or Scotopic Sensitivity. In adulthood, men and women who are LD still need certain kinds of help in order to succeed. Appendix A presents several excellent guidebooks that provide management strategies for teachers, workplace supervisors, and counselors who work with LD adults. Regardless of what type of learning disability is involved, the following management techniques are of critical importance for adults with learning disabilities.

EXTRA TIME

As this chapter has shown, too many brain pathways are incompletely formed to let the LD brain process information rapidly. Adults who are LD cannot speed up the rate at which their brains learn and remember. They must have extra time for reading, spelling, handwriting, math computation, answering questions, and understanding new information. As a rule, persons who are LD need three times longer than others to do their best in thinking things through, reading with full comprehension, writing what they know or think, and answering questions (Jordan, 1996a, 1996b, 1998). Pressure to make them hurry triggers cascades of frustration and awakens fearful memories.

Help with Reading

Adults who are dyslexic or have Scotopic Sensitivity must have help interpreting printed information. In the workplace, they should not be expected to read long memos or cope with complicated printed instructions. This is especially true when information is in small print. Someone who reads adequately should spend a few minutes with the LD adult, interpreting what printed materials say and mean. Hearing it instead of having to see it often allows LD adults to develop memory for what the printed data means. Then LD individuals can apply that information without being forced to struggle through the act of reading.

Help with Writing

Adults who are dyslexic and/or dysgraphic should not be expected to do much writing, especially by hand. Keyboard writing permits LD adults to express their knowledge much more fluently than handwriting. Adults with learning disabilities must have assistance in writing what they know. Speaking into a tape recorder in lieu of writing often satisfies job requirements or classroom assignments. Learning to use a word processor increases written expression 10 to 15 time compared with doing it by hand (Jordan, 1996a). Dictating essential information into a tape recorder or to a scribe allows LD adults to meet work quotas and classroom deadlines.

Using Hand Calculators

A hand calculator is a math keyboard. When adults have dyscalculia, or when thinking through math problems is extremely slow, using a calculator solves the problem of rapid math figuring. LD adults should carry small pocket calculators as faithfully as they carry keys and spending money.

Pocket Reminders

It is impossible for adults with LD to remember all of the important details of their lives. The simplest solution for forgetfulness is to carry pocket calendars that keep track of upcoming appointments and important engagements. LD adults must develop simple visual reminder systems that compensate for forgetfulness. A pocket calendar goes everywhere the person goes, in a shirt pocket, in a purse, or in a carryall bag. Learning to live by a pocket reminder is essential for LD individuals.

Help with Details

Every LD adult needs a friendly "supervisor" who reviews details with him or her several times each week. A spouse or mate, a friend, or a workplace partner can provide this gentle monitoring service. The purpose of having a "supervisor" is to make sure that no important details are ignored or forgotten. The person who monitors checks the pocket calendar to see that all obligations are jotted down. Money matters are reviewed to make sure that bills are paid on time and the checkbook is balanced. The heart of this assistance is to give positive support, not to criticize memory lapses.

Cortical Stimulant Medication

When attention deficits occur, the prefrontal cortex receives too little dopamine to keep the brain fully alert. Too little dopamine allows a condition called *underarousal* that makes the brain too "sleepy" to maintain full attention (Jordan, 1998). Three medications are specially tailored to increase the supply of dopamine to offset the influence of ADHD or ADD. *Ritalin* is the most frequently used cortical stimulant for ADD. In low to moderate dosage, Ritalin is one of the safest medications for increasing attention span. Sometimes Ritalin creates side effects, which means the person's brain chemistry is allergic to this medication. If so, *Cylert* often stabilizes the level of dopamine and increases attention span. A third cortical stimulant is *Adderal* which is a time-release version of an older medication Dexedrine. Adults with ADHD or ADD respond as well to these medications as do children and adolescents. Increasing dopamine in the prefrontal cortex can increase learning ability, improve job performance, and enhance memory for adults with residual ADD.

CHAPTER 2

How the Brain Learns and Remembers

Perhaps the most astonishing outcome of the Decade of the Brain was Antonio Damasio's discovery that the human brain does not begin to learn by absorbing facts. Instead, the brain starts the learning process by examining feelings and emotions (Damasio, 1994). Apparently we have been teaching backwards since formal education began.

HOW THE BRAIN RECEIVES NEW INFORMATION

Bloodstream

Long before the Decade of the Brain, mankind asked: How does the brain receive new information? The brain is securely sheltered inside a sturdy bone vault called the skull. A sea of fluid cushions the brain like a shock absorber. It is hoped that the brain never sees the light of day. How then, inside its bony fortress, does the brain learn what goes on in the outside world? Centuries ago scientists discovered the first principal information highway that delivers data to the brain: the bloodstream. This fluid system bathes every cell in the body, delivering nourishment and removing waste products. As it circulates through the brain, the bloodstream carries countless bits of chemical information that tell the brain how body cells are doing. The brain sends back other chemical messages that tell the cells what the brain needs for them to know. This flowing information highway deals largely with data about personal health, such as infections that may be developing, illnesses trying to take hold, and allergy attacks on body systems.

Viscera

Early scientists were aware of the central nervous system, but they were unsure what nerve fibers throughout the body had to do with the brain. The Decade of the Brain finished answering that question. Hanna and Antonio Damasio at the University of Iowa (Damasio, 1994), Daniel Schacter at Harvard University (Schacter, 1996), and others have described how the extremely complex nerve network throughout the body brings new information to the brain. In addition to receiving constant new data from the bloodstream, the brain also receives sensory information through the *viscera*. The viscera refers to the entire skin on the outside of the body, as well as to all of the organs inside the body cavity. Every bit of skin contains nerve endings that fire outside information to the brain: temperature, pressure, texture, odors, sounds, what the eyes see, and so forth. The viscera also relays inside data about the digestive tract, heartbeat, breathing, taste, need to eliminate, and when it is time to eat. The bloodstream and viscera bombard the brain with millions of bits of data that must be sorted out and responded to.

CENTRAL NERVOUS SYSTEM

Figure 2.1 shows details of neuron chains that fire new information along nerve lines called *axon pathways.* These axon pathways gather data from every part of the viscera and bring it to the brain. Axon pathways also deliver messages from the brain to all parts of the body. Some axon pathways are very small, only a few molecules in length. Others are long enough to reach several inches from the front of the brain down to the brain stem. Millions of axon pathways bind together to create the "gray matter" of the brain. Other axons follow the outside curves of the brain to create the cortex where learning and memory take place.

LEARNING DISABLED BRAIN PATHWAYS

When learning disabilities exist, many axon pathways fail to develop fully. These structural differences interrupt signals that

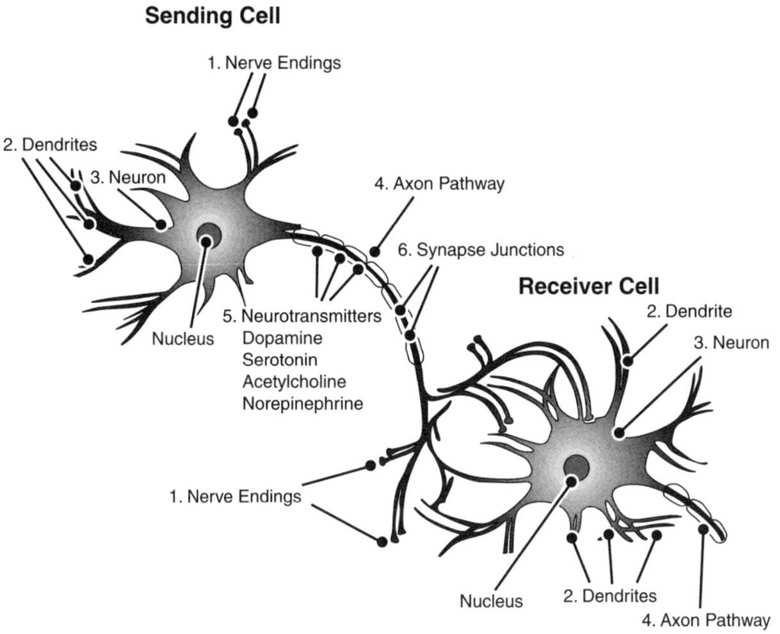

Sending Cell

1. Nerve Endings

2. Dendrites

3. Neuron

4. Axon Pathway

6. Synapse Junctions

Receiver Cell

5. Neurotransmitters
Dopamine
Serotonin
Acetylcholine
Norepinephrine

2. Dendrite

3. Neuron

Nucleus

1. Nerve Endings

Nucleus   2. Dendrites

4. Axon Pathway

Figure 2.1. Nerve endings in the skin (1) pick up new information from out-side the body and send it along dendrites (2) into the neuron (3). This information is then sent down the axon pathway (4) by neurotransmitters (5) that fire from one synapse junction (6) to the next until the message reaches the receiver cell. This chain of events is repeated until the new information reaches the brain stem.

travel between neurons. Figure 2.2 shows the four-step developmental sequence all brain cells must follow if they are to become part of the axon pathway system. New brain cells sprout a thicket of connectors called *dendrites*. Each dendrite could become a connecting link with another cell. However, the brain regulates the number of dendrites by pruning away extra ones the brain does not intend to use. This produces a streamlined central nervous system that transmits information on schedule with no interference. When LD exists, too many unnecessary dendrites remain. These extra dendrites cause brain messages and thought patterns to scramble and move down wrong axon pathways. Unpruned dendrites contribute to dyslexia, Scotopic Sensitivity syndrome, and attention deficit disorders described in Chapter 1.

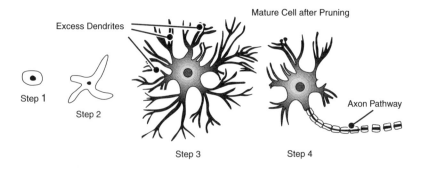

Figure 2.2. Brain cells must go through a four-step developmental sequence in order to take part in brain processing. Learning disabilities are found when brain cells do not finish Step 3. As new cells begin to connect to other cell clusters, unnecessary dendrites are pruned away. When too many dendrites remain (are not pruned away), the brain cannot develop good thought processing. Too many dendrites allow thought patterns to scatter instead of becoming focused.

BRAIN STEM FILTERING

It would be impossible for the brain to process all of the new information it receives from the bloodstream and viscera. To protect the higher brain from data overload, the brain stem sifts through all new information first. The midbrain, or *limbic system,* is an incredibly complex system that is designed to filter out unnecessary information from the viscera. Figure 2.3 shows the sequence that all axon pathway data takes before it reaches the higher brain. In fractions of a second, the brain stem selects information that should be considered by the higher brain. Irrelevant or unnecessary data is filtered out and discarded. Important information then passes upward to the *cerebellum* and *medulla.* The cerebellum reviews all data that is related to movement of the body or parts of the body. The cerebellum rapidly organizes this nonverbal data into "bundles" that are sent on to the *thalamus.* The medulla sorts and organizes incoming data that is related to verbal issues. These verbal bundles are fired on to the *hippocampus.* The hippocampus determines which verbal data should become part of the higher brain's memory. This potential memory information is fired up

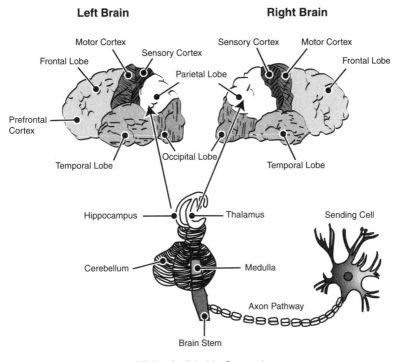

Left Brain **Right Brain**

Motor Cortex

Sensory Cortex

Frontal Lobe

Parietal Lobe

Sensory Cortex Motor Cortex

Frontal Lobe

Prefrontal Cortex

Temporal Lobe

Occipital Lobe

Temporal Lobe

Hippocampus Thalamus

Sending Cell

Cerebellum Medulla

Axon Pathway

Brain Stem

Midbrain (Limbic System)

Figure 2.3. All new information comes first to the *brain stem* where it is filtered. Unnecessary data that the brain does not need to know is discarded. This filtered data moves up through the *cerebellum* and *medulla* where it is further filtered and preorganized. Language-based information is sent to the *hippocampus* which decides what part of this data should enter the higher brain memory centers. Nonverbal information is sent to the *thalamus* which sorts out the data that should go to higher brain centers. Then this filtered, organized information is fired to the *parietal lobes* which sort out each type of data (visual, auditory, sensory, motor) and transfer that information to the correct region of the higher brain.

to the *left parietal lobe* which classifies new data "bundles" according to what they tell. Visual data is fired to the *occipital lobe*. Auditory data is sent to the *temporal lobe*. Information related to logical thinking is transferred to the *prefrontal cortex*. Important data to be remembered later is forwarded to the *frontal lobe*. Meanwhile, the *right parietal lobe* receives incoming nonverbal data from the thalamus. Data related to smell, touch, taste, or feeling is delivered to the *sensory cortex*. Information related to motion and body movement is sent to the *motor cortex*.

LD BRAIN PATHWAYS

Individuals with learning disabilities have many underdeveloped nerve pathways that interrupt the filtering, organizing, and forwarding of new data between the brain stem and higher brain regions. When dyslexia exists, the left visual cortex cannot learn which direction symbols should face or the right sequence of symbols. When auditory dyslexia occurs, incomplete cell development in the medial geniculate nucleus and left auditory pathway fails to process the hard/fast, soft/slow sounds of speech. When Scotopic Sensitivity syndrome exists, underdeveloped cells along the magnicellular visual pathway deliver distorted images to the midbrain and visual cortex. The Decade of the Brain has revealed how differences in brain structure cause learning disabilities that keep bright individuals from becoming fully educated.

EMOTIONS AND THE BRAIN

Neurotransmitters

Research by Damasio, Ratey and Johnson, Schacter, Shapiro and others have described the chemical and neuronal components of the left brain and midbrain that govern expression of emotion (Damasio, 1994; Ratey & Johnson, 1997; Schacter, 1996; Shapiro, 1995). Figure 2.1 lists four main neurotransmitters that are involved in cell firing and axon pathway transmissions. These neurotransmitters also play a key role in the brain's balance of emotions. *Dopamine* helps to regulate the alertness (arousal) of the brain, especially the prefrontal cortex. This is a critical part in paying full attention. Dopamine also tells the sensory cortex when the person has had enough sensual pleasure and stimulation. Dopamine is part of the brain chemistry team that causes the person to feel rewarded and satisfied. *Serotonin* soothes strong urges that originate in the limbic system. When the midbrain impulse wants to "do it now, not later," or when anxiety or panic is about to break loose, serotonin helps the brain keep such urges under control. *Norepinephrine* teams with serotonin and dopamine to push depression away. Without enough norepinephrine, an individual sinks into depression states, such as SAD (Seasonal Affective Disorder) and monopolar depression that are described in Chapter 5. *Acetylcholine* helps to regulate short-term and long-term memory. This team of neurotransmitters maintains inner peace, logical thinking, and waiting patiently before acting.

Centers of Emotion: Executive Function

Figure 2.4 shows the emotion control centers of the limbic system and the prefrontal cortex. When the brain is developed normally with neurotransmitters in good balance, the prefrontal cortex stays in charge through logical thinking and cause/effect reasoning. This in-charge process often is called *executive function.* Like an executive in charge of a group, the prefrontal cortex is the seat of higher "social emotions," such as patience, kindness, joy, peace, compassion, tolerance, affection, and compassion. The executive prefrontal cortex is the mature "parent" whose principal function is to say "Wait!" to the rest of the brain. "Wait. Not yet. Let's think this through. What will the consequences be if we act now, or if we decide not to act at all?" The prefrontal cortex presides over the brain's inner voice that allows various regions to contribute information. The executive function of the prefrontal cortex maintains order and emotional discipline with impulses under control. The prefrontal cortex is the wise, patient, mature "parent who lives upstairs."

"Downstairs" in the limbic system live our strong emotional "children" who disrupt our lives through antisocial behavior. Figure 2.4 shows the amygdala which is the center for such disruptive emotions as aggression, rage, lust, jealousy, fear, suspicion, anger, hostility, desire for revenge, anxiety, panic, terror,

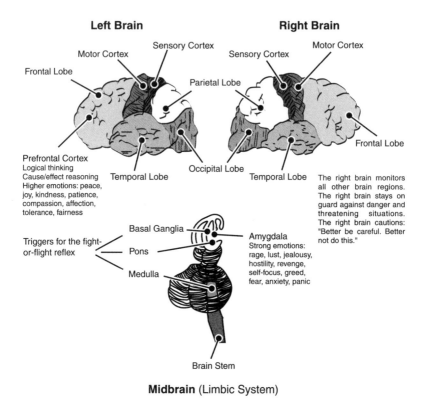

Left Brain

Right Brain

Sensory Cortex

Motor Cortex

Sensory Cortex

Motor Cortex

Frontal Lobe

Parietal Lobe

Frontal Lobe

Prefrontal Cortex
Logical thinking
Cause/effect reasoning
Higher emotions: peace,
joy, kindness, patience,
compassion, affection,
tolerance, fairness

Temporal Lobe

Occipital Lobe

Temporal Lobe

The right brain monitors
all other brain regions.
The right brain stays on
guard against danger and
threatening situations.
The right brain cautions:
"Better be careful. Better
not do this."

Basal Ganglia

Amygdala
Strong emotions:
rage, lust, jealousy,
hostility, revenge,
self-focus, greed,
fear, anxiety, panic

Triggers for the fight-
or-flight reflex

Pons

Medulla

Brain Stem

Midbrain (Limbic System)

Figure 2.4. Higher emotions originate in the *prefrontal cortex* where the left brain uses logical thinking and cause/effect reasoning to solve problems. Strong, destructive emotions originate in the brain stem and the *amygdala.* Three other midbrain regions (*pons, medulla,* and *basal ganglia*) team together to trigger the fight-or-flight reflex when the brain stem signals possible danger. Many LD adults live under the control of fears that keep the fight-or-flight reflex on high alert along with surges of strong emotions from the amygdala. These individuals have very little peace in their lives.

greed, and self-focus. These destructive emotions clamor to act now. The "emotional children" in the amygdala care nothing about waiting. "Let's do it now! Forget about waiting! It's too boring to wait." In a healthy brain with neurotransmitters in good balance, the prefrontal cortex stays in charge. When axon pathways are intact and neurotransmitters are balanced, individuals learn over time to say "no" and "not yet" to their urges.

LD AND EMOTIONS

A major problem for LD adults is staying in logical control of strong emotions. An earmark of learning disability is impatience that drives the impulse to "do it now!" Adults who are LD often struggle not to lose their temper or explode in a tantrum. Postponing a desire is a major challenge, especially when hyperactivity and attention deficit (ADHD) overlap dyslexia. It is not easy for an LD adult to remember the sequence while thinking through a complicated situation. Putting off pleasure can be too difficult for an LD adult who throws a party on payday instead of saving back enough for the rent. Chapter 5 describes several "shadow syndromes" that hide behind dyslexia, ADHD, and ADD. These hidden problems frequently are related to imbalance of brain chemistry when dopamine and serotonin are in short supply. Along with the invisible struggles of LD, adults with learning disabilities always are on the edge of emotional upset. In fact, part of being LD is the lifelong inner battle over whether emotions will control one's life.

THE LANGUAGE OF THE BRAIN

Firing Rhythms

The Decade of the Brain discovered that all of the regions of the brain communicate through electrical pulses called *firing rhythms,* or *timing rhythms.* Rodolfo Llinas at Massachusetts Institute of Technology measured the speed of cell firing in different regions of the brain (Llinas, 1993). He discovered that brain stem cells fire steadily at the rate of 10 cycles per second. This firing rhythm creates a "fluid-like motion" of electrical activity that transmits data throughout the limbic system and up to the higher brain. Llinas also measured cell-firing rates in the higher brain. For example, he discovered that the prefrontal cortex, which governs other brain activity the way an executive controls an organization, has different rates of cell firing. During deep sleep, the prefrontal cortex shuts down its governing functions and fires at 2 cycles per second. As the prefrontal cortex begins to wake up, cell firing increases to 10 cycles per second. When the brain is fully aroused and alert, the prefrontal cortex fires at 40 cycles per second.

Inner Voice

These cell-firing rhythms create an *inner voice* much like a radar system fires energy waves toward the horizon, then receives echoes that bring data back to home base. When the brain is well developed and functioning normally, the inner voice communicates in quiet rhythms, much like the harmonic "humming" we hear in recordings of whales as they communicate underwater. When learning disabilities exist, the brain does not have a consistent, rhythmical inner voice. Extra dendrites and underdeveloped neurons create "inner static" the way lightning interferes with television and radio broadcasts. The inner voice of an LD brain is more like noise than a steady rhythm. In their book *Shadow Syndromes,* John Ratey and Catherine Johnson call this the "noisy brain" (Ratey & Johnson, 1997). Learning disabilities make it impossible for LD individuals to process language or do other types of thinking without continual mistakes in brain language transmission.

HOW THE BRAIN REMEMBERS

Is This Safe?

In his book *Descartes' Error,* Damasio describes the critical role that emotions and feelings play in how the brain learns and remembers (Damasio, 1994). According to Damasio's model, the brain stem stands guard over personal safety. All new data that arrives at the brain stem is compared instantly with what the higher brain already knows. Figure 2.5 shows Damasio's model

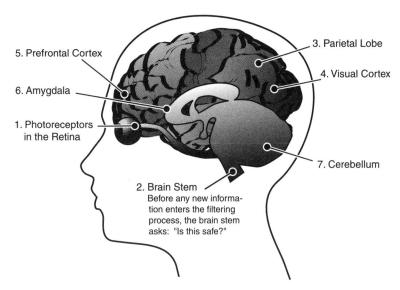

1. The eyes (1) see something new or different. This visual data is flashed to the brain stem (2), then to the parietal lobe (3), and finally to the visual cortex (4).

2. The visual cortex simultaneously flashes that data to the prefrontal cortex (5) and the amygdala (6).

3. The prefrontal cortex starts the process of interpreting what the eyes have just seen. At the same time, the amygdala signals the right brain and cerebellum (7) that possible danger may exist. The amygdala, cerebellum, and right brain go on full alert.

4. The amygdala, cerebellum, and right brain wait for the prefrontal cortex to decide if this situation is safe, or if the person faces danger (fight-or-flight reflex).

5. The prefrontal cortex does a rapid check of past experiences like this new one. If past experience has been safe, the prefrontal cortex sends an "all clear" signal that lets the cerebellum and amygdala relax. The person continues as if nothing has happened.

6. If the prefrontal cortex discovers an old memory of danger related to this new visual data, the signal is flashed to the brain stem to attack (fight) or to run or avoid (flight).

Figure 2.5. Damasio has described this six-step process that the brain follows to decide which emotions and feelings will become part of every permanent memory. This model applies to all moments of hearing, smelling, touching, tasting, and seeing. The brain's first response to new data is to check out the level of safety, or level of threat. After emotions and feelings have been analyzed, then the higher brain deals with facts that are related to new information. (Damasio 1995)

of how the brain processes new data according to whether it is safe. The issue of safety is especially critical for those who have learning disabilities. Because so many language experiences have been difficult since early childhood, LD adults are loaded with negative memories related to classroom learning, reading, writing tasks, following instructions, and trying something new. In fact, many LD adults have active phobias related to school performance, entering a classroom, doing written assignments, taking tests, or reading aloud before others.

Engrams

During the Decade of the Brain, Daniel Schacter at Harvard School of Medicine developed a model of how the brain stores events as long-term memory. In his book *Searching for Memory*, Schacter describes the process that produces *engrams,* his name for "memory molecules" that exist throughout the brain hemispheres (Schacter, 1996). Figure 2.6 shows this model of memory development. An engram is something like a sandwich with a fact nestled inside the emotions and feelings that occurred when the brain learned that fact. Schacter's engram model explains why we often are surprised by a vivid memory we had not thought of in many years. An odor, a scene, a sound, or a human voice often trigger these memory surprises. "Now why did I think of that?" we ask ourselves. Schacter explains that a sensory event, such as the odor of a fresh apple pie, awakens a dormant engram that was formed early in life but was not activated until now.

HOW ENGRAMS ARE FORMED

One recent day I watched as a series of vivid engrams were implanted in the lifelong memory of a small child. I was waiting in the airport terminal for a friend to arrive. As I waited, I looked at a beautiful speedboat on display in the corridor. After enjoying some pleasant daydreams about what if that boat were mine, I wandered away toward the arrival gate. Suddenly the corridor was filled with the horrified screams of a badly frightened child.

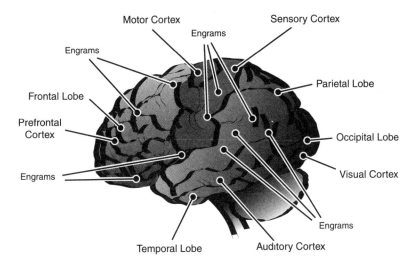

Figure 2.6. Scattered throughout the higher brain are countless molecules where bundles of memory materials are stored as codes. Schacter has called these memory codes "engrams." An engram is much like a sandwich with a fact embedded inside the emotions and feelings that existed when that fact was learned. Engrams may remain dormant for many years. A new event similar to an old one triggers the brain to search for that old memory. Suddenly the original emotions and feelings come alive. Schacter's model of engram development suggests that every learning experience is stored in the brain with facts wrapped inside original emotions and feelings. Unexpected odors, sounds, or sights can awaken old engrams after many years of being inactive. (Schacter 1997)

As a father and grandfather, I knew very well what that piercing shriek meant. A young child was caught in the grip of total fear. Everyone turned to look. Inside the boat was a terrified little boy about 2 years old. As a way of teaching his grandson some facts about boats, his grandfather had lifted the little fellow into the boat. "Look at that steering wheel, Johnny," Grandad said. "Hey, look at those fancy seats." But Johnny's brain was not dealing with Grandad's facts. Instead, this child's brain was overwhelmed by strong, destructive emotions and feelings. As soon as he could catch his breath, Johnny wailed "Water! Water!" I knew what his imagination was seeing. Johnny's limbic system was convinced that he was about to tumble out of the boat into water. "There's no water," Grandad explained. Another fact for his grandson to learn. But Johnny's prefrontal cortex had lost the battle for logical control. The terrified child had a white-knuckle grip on the edge of the boat to keep from falling into the water.

As Grandad finally lifted the little boy out of that frightening situation, I thought of what was taking place inside Johnny's young brain. According to Schacter's model, fresh engrams were forming that will live in this child's memory the rest of his life. Suppose that someday Grandad takes Johnny by the hand and says: "Come on, let's get in my boat and go fishing." With no warning, this grandchild will have a panic attack. Instantly the fearful engrams implanted by that "daymare" in the airport terminal will come alive. For the rest of his childhood, and possibly his adulthood, Johnny will be afraid of boats, yet he may not remember why. This kind of nightmare memory can be triggered without warning by something Johnny sees, hears, or smells someday. As Schacter explains, we never learn a fact by itself. The brain wraps all remembered facts inside emotions and feelings called engrams. These sleeping molecules of coded memory come alive anytime we have a new experience that reminds the brain of an old moment that threatened our safety.

We also develop engrams of joyful times. Early one Saturday morning I began a 2-hour drive to a campus where I taught a graduate class in adult education. This always was a pleasant drive that let me watch the sun rise, listen to favorite music, and prepare my brain for the day. I was half-listening to the radio when suddenly I heard the opening bars of Tchaikovsky's overture to *Romeo and Juliet*. To my astonishment, I began to cry. Deep sobs filled my eyes with tears. What on earth was happening to me?

Then I remembered an early morning 43 years ago when I had listened to *Romeo and Juliet*. I was a young soldier in the American army stationed overseas. I was extremely lonely for my wife who was about to give birth to our first child, and I was thousands of miles from home. One night I was awakened and told that an overseas telephone call had come for me. I hurried to the phone to learn that our daughter had been born. With mixed emotions I dressed and walked to the dayroom on our army base. There was a small lounge with a phonograph and some scratchy old albums of classical music. As I sat down to write a love letter to my wife and new daughter, the opening bars of *Romeo and Juliet* began to play. That early morning so long ago, I burst into tears of joy. For 43 years that engram lay dormant in my brain to be awakened without warning as I heard familiar music during an early morning drive.

ENGRAMS OF LEARNING DISABILITIES

In view of Damasio's and Schacter's explanations of how the brain starts with emotions and feelings, not with facts, it is important to understand the impact of old fear engrams when LD adults approach formal learning. Figure 2.5 shows Damasio's model of how the brain checks for safety as new data enters the brain. Step 6 in Figure 2.5 becomes critical when LD adults come back to school. If the early years of classroom learning were filled with failure, pain, embarrassment, and trauma, then the brain is filled with old fear engrams of early learning. Suppose a 7-year-old child is dyslexic and cannot make sense of printed symbols, or is "tone deaf" in listening. Countless times that child is scolded, shamed, reprimanded, ridiculed, and even punished for not doing better. No matter how hard this LD child tries, he or she cannot build good literacy skills. Each moment of failure wraps that fact inside strong emotions and feelings of anger, fear, hostility, and desire for revenge. Suppose that at age 33 this grown-up child decides to enter an adult education program to earn a GED (General Education Development) diploma or increase reading ability for job promotion. What if this LD adult walks into an evening classroom that looks like those school rooms where he or she failed? Without warning, old engrams will be activated with all of those strong, negative emotions and feelings now wide awake. Suddenly this LD adult is on full alert, consumed by old fear, anger, and humiliation. However, suppose that he or she is mature enough to overcome that strong surge of old memories about school. What if this LD adult is ushered into a room and asked to take a reading test so the instructor will know where to start with skill development? Suddenly this school-phobic adult has a panic attack. Blood pressure surges. Heartbeat accelerates. Skin begins to sweat. Breathing becomes labored. Most of all, fear escalates beyond control. This stricken adult races out of that place and may never return to continuing education.

CHAPTER 3

Nonverbal Learning Disability in Adults

PROBLEMS WITH THE LD LABEL

Communication problems often occur when the term LD is used. Chapter 1 describes four current meanings of the label LD. When educators discuss LD, they can mean the struggle to learn in the classroom, or the types of behavior that disrupt personal lives and group activities, or the late physical maturity that creates immature lifestyles. The label LD includes problems with academic learning as well as disruptive social behavior.

NONVERBAL LEARNING DISABILITY: NVLD

Several years before the Decade of the Brain, specialists in specific learning disabilities began to notice social struggles in adolescents and adults who could not learn to "dance the tribal dance" of their families, communities, or cultures. After years of training in social skills, these older persons remained socially awkward, even crude in personal relationships. In the early 1970s Doris Johnson and Helmut Myklebust described a cluster of irregular social behaviors they named *Nonverbal Learning Disabilities* [NVLD] (Johnson & Myklebust, 1971). Individuals with NVLD display a "lifestyle disability" that makes it impossible for them to get the meaning of what goes on around them socially. For example, NVLD persons do not understand social humor. They rarely get the point of jokes or gentle teasing. They have great difficulty entering into make-believe or "let's pretend" activities. Individuals with NVLD are very poor at paying attention outside themselves. They remain self-focused all their lives. They cannot anticipate what is coming next by reading body language or by gleaning cues from social conversation. In the 1980s the term *social disability* was coined to describe individuals who cannot read social signals, such as facial expressions, hand gestures, body language, friendly touching, and tone of voice (Jordan, 1989).

RIGHT-HEMISPHERE LD

In 1974 Daniel Tranel suggested that lesions in the right brain might contribute to NVLD behavior. Eventually Tranel and his colleagues named this condition *Right-Hemisphere Learning Disability* (Tranel et al., 1987). During the Decade of the Brain, Vilayanur Ramachandran at the University of California in San Diego discovered "blister-like bubbles" along axon pathways in the right brains of adults who have trouble with social skills (Ramachandran, 1993). He called these lesions *Unidentified Bright Objects* (UBOs.) Tiny breaks in the myelin sheath that surrounds each axon segment become filled with fluid. On brain scans these lesions shine like "bright objects in space." Individuals with UBOs along right brain pathways display "social disability" in their behavior.

Right-Hemisphere LD creates lifelong problems getting along with others. These adolescents and adults are misfits in classroom settings. They cannot get along with teachers and others in authority. They rarely do well in the workplace. Right-Hemisphere LD fosters negative attitudes that include a lot of complaining and blaming others. These individuals are unpleasant to be with day after day. Their irregular, negative behavior triggers undercurrents of conflict that causes them to be unpopular. Most adults with Right-Hemisphere LD drift from job to job, and from relationship to relationship. They are poor partners in marriage and have little success as parents. These individuals rarely make positive comments. In fact, they habitually make negative criticisms and "put down" comments intended to make others feel less sure of themselves. As an NVLD adult said to me: "Everyone has to look down on somebody." Right-Hemisphere LD is not an academic issue. Instead, those individuals spend their lives finding fault, blaming others, and stirring up hard feelings in every relationship. This is the way they see the world around them. They do not tune in to positive issues that must exist if social groups are to succeed.

AUTISTIC SPECTRUM SYNDROME

To understand Nonverbal LD more fully, we must review the neurological syndrome called *autism*. Figure 3.1 shows the regions of the brain that continually communicate with each other to share information, interpret new data, update memory by adding new data, make decisions, and control emotions and feelings. Chapter 2 describes the language of the brain, the fluent "electrical flow" that streams back and forth among all of the brain regions. In normally developed brains, axon pathways carry brain messages the way fiber-optic cables transmit voice messages around the world. When autism exists, major brain regions are cut off from each other. Visual information from the occipital lobe does not connect with tactile information from the motor cortex. Auditory information from the temporal lobe does not connect with visual data from the visual cortex. Sometimes autistic adults develop the ability to describe what it is like being autistic. Visual images are so distorted the person does not recognize faces, shapes, or line patterns. Speech sounds are distorted into frightening screeches or overpowering booms and hisses. Frontal lobes receive bizarre memory material that is more like fantasy than reality. Most individuals who are autistic are bombarded by exaggerated impressions, such as acutely sensitive skin sensations, amplified sounds, sudden emotional surges, overpowering feelings, and monster-like mental images that startle and alarm.

Like all syndromes, autism is seen along a range from mild to severe:

1	2	3		4	5	6	7		8	9	10
	mild				moderate					severe	

The most severe forms of autism make it impossible for outsiders to communicate with persons who are autistic. Level 9 and 10

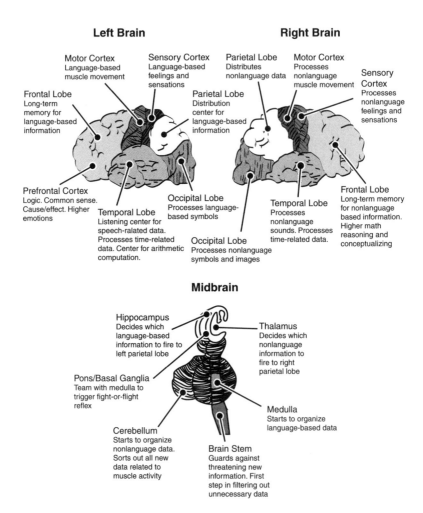

Figure 3.1. All of these brain regions constantly communicate in order to maintain attention, deal with new events, make decisions, upgrade memory data, recall what has been learned, regulate emotions and feelings, and so forth. Autism occurs when major axon links are missing between brain centers. This isolates important brain centers, making it impossible for them to communicate with each other.

autism disrupts brain functions so severely that this individual is beyond the reach of language or touch. Less severe autism (Level 7 or 8) permits limited degrees of communication, so long as outsiders approach quietly, gently, and without unexpected touching. Over time, a severely autistic child might move down the severity scale to moderate levels of impairment (Level 5 or 6) by adulthood. Autism often involves late development of axon pathways between brain regions. This allows "late bloomers" eventually to cross communication barriers as neuronal maturity occurs inside the brain.

HIGH FUNCTIONING AUTISM

Often we find persons with low moderate (Level 4) or mild (Level 3) autism. This is called *high functioning autism.* A popular example is the autistic math genius in the movie *Rain Man.* He required daily supervision to bathe and eat regularly, yet he had genius-level talent in mental arithmetic. In such a person, axon pathways are functional between some of the major brain centers. This allows the individual to display extraordinary talent for music, reading, mathematics, or memory for trivial details. This kind of limited, highly specialized use of intelligence is called *autistic savant.*

Chapter 1 describes the Irlen procedure which applies color, or a combination of colors, to the visual processing of individuals who are "word blind" (Scotopic Sensitivity syndrome). During the Decade of the Brain, I was consultant to a research project sponsored by the Irlen Institute in Long Beach, California. This project worked with high-functioning autistic adults to see if adding color might reduce visual distortion enough to teach these intelligent persons to read. During the course of that project, I received an essay from a 38-year-old autistic man in England. I know him only as Paul. He wanted to tell others about the dramatic difference that color makes in his perception of the world around him. Below is part of his articulate description just as he wrote it of what it is like to be autistic:

> Everything I ever saw throughout my life was in such fine detail. If I stood in a room and looked down I would see the material, the weave, the colors, the order, the structure of the carpet. Within the structure I would see two

giant islands which were my feet with toes and heels always lining up per-fectly, sending invisible lines firing across the order of the carpet at right angles. I was forever moving and lining up, making sure my feet and those invisible lines made by my feet blended into the surroundings. I didn't see the carpet because the order and the structure and the pattern of the carpet were so bombarding, I couldn't see the whole object.

Now with my colored glasses I see this carpet. I see it's the floor, the base of the room, the available walking space. I can see its function. Before the glasses, this carpet was just a void, a large space that seemed to go on for a long time with various obstructions like chairs and walls seem-ing to be in the distance. I constantly plotted lines and angles and dis-tances just to be able to know where everything was, including myself.

This constant mapping and drawing out and lining of a room or a ceiling or a wall or a garden or a street or a classroom full of moving chil-dren and changing blackboard marks and echoing teachers' voices took so much energy and constant attention that it robbed me of learning, of understanding, of hearing a single sound source on its own. People's talk-ing would become the rhythms and I would lose the meaning of the words. I had very little control of the focus of what I saw and heard. I could never see and hear at the same time. I had no way of understanding what other people were doing unless I focused entirely upon that single person, thereby tuning out all the mapping and all the constant visual re-construction of my surroundings. Either I was in a world that I was so scared and unsure of and had very little understanding in, or I left the world and became the object of my attention.

At an early age, I learned to mimic and copy other people. This gave me at least some kind of feeling of normality. Through this I began to have my first social-emotional experiences, but these experiences were fearful and lacked any happiness or joy because I lacked understanding of what was happening. This fear was caused by being out of control of what was happening to me.

Then I got these colored glasses. I can read with meaning and still be aware of things happening around me. I can walk in a room and see the entire floor space and chairs and walls and ceiling as one large box that I'm inside. Before these glasses, I would see hundreds of individual blades of grass, all twisting their own way, each shaped unlike the others. But now I see the grass and I see a lawn and the flower boarders and the fences as one whole picture. I see people now as other living whole creatures and they're not as threatening as they used to.

VERY HIGH FUNCTIONING AUTISM: RIGHT-HEMI SYNDROME

During the 1970s Martha Denckla at Johns Hopkins School of Medicine described a type of learning disability that involved lifelong difficulties with social skills, similar to Nonverbal Learning Disability (Denckla, 1978). Denckla suggested that this form of LD is linked to very high functioning autism. Drake Duane, a neurologist at the Mayo Clinic, extended the research of Tranel and Denckla by proposing what he called *Right-Hemi syndrome* (Duane, 1985). Persons with Right-Hemi syndrome might be well educated, but they display the following mildly autistic habits:

1. Avoiding eye contact during conversation
2. Speaking in a sing-song fashion (prosody)
3. Smothering others through overly possessive attitudes
4. Making inappropriate displays of affection
5. Triggering dread in others
6. Being blind to normal social signals
7. Ignoring privacy signals from others
8. Ignoring signals to stay out of the personal space of others
9. Speaking inappropriately (blurting out, butting in)

It is easy to see why such an individual has difficulty in the workplace and in personal relationships. In spite of adequate education or job skill training, this person gets along poorly with others. He or she is frequently in conflict with supervisors and other authority figures. Individuals with Right-Hemi syndrome have few friends because of overbearing possessiveness and jealousy. Their social conduct is crude, self-focused, and often inappropriate. These individuals continually trigger arguments and disagreements, which makes them unpopular targets for rejection.

VERY HIGH FUNCTIONING AUTISM:
ASPERGER'S SYNDROME

During the 1980s, several specialists in LD followed Denckla's lead by researching the link between irregular social behavior and autism. Major emphasis was placed upon exploring *Asperger's syndrome.* In 1994 the fourth edition of the *Diagnostic and Statistical Manual* (*DSM IV*) of the American Psychiatric Association included Asperger's syndrome as a type of psychological disability called *Pervasive Developmental Disorder*

(American Psychiatric Association, 1994). In the book *Attention Deficit Disorder: ADHD and ADD Syndromes,* I describe 19 symptoms of Asperger's syndrome (Jordan, 1998):

1. Awkward lifelong gross motor coordination
2. Boring, flat tone of voice
3. Failure to read social signals
4. Awkwardness at making small talk
5. Slowness in thinking and responding
6. Excellent recall of some area of trivial details
7. Restricted sense of humor
8. Narrow range of interests
9. Obsessive hair splitting and arguing about details
10. Effect of triggering dread in others
11. Inappropriate social habits
12. Obsessive/compulsive ritualized behavior
13. Passive/aggressive stubbornness
14. Aggressive control of others
15. Boring personality
16. Automatic rationalizing (explaining away own responsibility)
17. High degree of creativity within a narrow range of talent
18. Inability to work well with others
19. Poor leadership ability

Lifelong Impact of Asperger's Syndrome

Trouble Finding Work

It is a great irony that many adults with Asperger's syndrome are well educated, often with advanced degrees in medicine, education, science, engineering, philosophy, mathematics, or the law. Yet they often have difficulty finding work or developing romantic relationships. Job interviews implant the impression that "we don't want this weird person on our staff." If Asperger's individuals are employed, their disruptive "lifestyle disability" seldom fits into groups. In fact, their irregular, boring habits and eccentric lifestyles alienate them from mainstream relationships. Adults with Asperger's syndrome usually are excluded by peers and colleagues who find their behavior to be "weird," "strange," "bizarre," "eccentric," or even "obnoxious." On the job, they split hairs endlessly and argue over trivial issues to the point of angering associates. In a marriage or dating relationship, they are overly possessive and jealous. Most adults with Asperger's syndrome are lonely. They do not understand why they are rejected or scorned by others. This type of LD is an unfortunate disability because high intelligence and creativity often do not find success in the workplace. Personal relationships are filled with conflict that is triggered by inappropriate behavior. An Asperger's syndrome adult rarely finds romantic love. He or she is too "strange" to permit normal affection to develop with others.

Inflexible Leadership

Occasionally an Asperger's person becomes a department leader or group supervisor in the workplace. This occurs when an institution promotes according to years in service or by high scores on job placement tests. As a supervisor, an Asperger's person becomes a rigid boss who enforces rules and regulations without regard to human differences or extenuating circumstances. Such a leader becomes tyrannical in applying and interpreting workplace rules. He or she never accepts responsibility for mistakes or problems in the workplace. Instead, the Asperger's leader blames colleagues. This kind of rigid, irrational leadership triggers low morale among subordinates who are offended by insensitive treatment from above. A great deal of workplace misery follows the appointment of an Asperger's individual to a position of authority.

Excessive Communication

During my four decades working with LD adolescents and adults, I have known many persons with Asperger's syndrome. Because I am kind and patient with them, these lonely ones often form strong attachments to me. Frequently an Asperger's individual begins to correspond with me. As one intelligent Asperger's man wrote: "It is easier for me to express myself in writing. Putting words on paper gives me enough time to think through what I want to tell you." A stunning habit of many Asperger's adults is the length of their letters, FAX memos, and e-mail messages. An earmark of Asperger's syndrome is the compulsion to go into far greater detail than others want to hear or read. My Asperger's friends rarely send letters of one or two pages. Usually they send correspondence of a dozen or more pages typed single space. One lonely adult sent a handwritten 53-page letter to me. A bright man with Asperger's syndrome asked me to look over his application for graduate school. The application form provided half a page for a brief autobiographical summary. The Asperger's individual had attached a 14-page autobiography, typed single space, because he could not give just the main points of his life.

Below is an example of the emotional and intellectual content of a letter I received from an Asperger's syndrome man, now deceased. The letter was written in a spiral notebook, then ripped out with no thought of trimming off the ragged left edge. His writing filled every inch of space, crowding the edges and filling space between lines he had already written. In spite of having a college degree, he was unaware of the social etiquette of letter writing.

> Dr. Jordan:
> Hi! I'm a learning-disabled journalist, turning 38 shortly. I'm writing to thank you for your book ADD. The *symptoms checklists* are *great*! I *especially* appreciate the symptoms of "immaturity" and "lack of continuity." I have a B.A. from a state university 3.2 GPA for (public) high school and college. I've interviewed with the *Los Angeles Times* and worked all shifts for a wire service, *et al.* I've played piano since age six. I've never had a sweetheart or been in a boyfriend-girlfriend relationship. I *do want* to marry. But I still live with my parents, unfortunately. I also benefit from books such as "Undressing the American Male" by Eva Margolles, and "Shyness and Love" by Brian Gilmartin. I've written several screenplays during the past decade—inspired in large part by my high-school, university and journalism experiences. I haven't had anything produced *yet,* but I'm *determined* to get an agent. Your teacher-training workshops sound valuable. I'd like to do similar events—e.g., speak to corporate/business 'Human Resources' gatherings. I certainly advocate *inclusion* for people like me!

This rambling style of writing that includes grandiose, unrealistic wishes (lecture to corporate executives, become famous as a screenwriter) is typical of many adults with Asperger's syndrome. As Duane indicated in his Right-Hemi syndrome model,

Asperger's adults often are well educated, but they cannot find work in their stated area of expertise. In our culture, many Asperger's syndrome adults continue to live with aging parents because they cannot achieve independence. This is a characteristic of autism, even at a very high functioning level.

How Severe Is Asperger's Syndrome?

Chapter 1 presents the need to determine how severe a syndrome is before we can discuss its impact. To estimate the impact of Asperger's syndrome in adulthood, we must consider levels of severity in different persons. Appendix B presents the *Jordan Index for Asperger's Syndrome* that is designed to estimate individual levels of severity. It is unlikely that an adult with Asperger's symptoms could do this index as a self-evaluation activity. A major deficit of Asperger's is the inability to see one's self objectively. This index is intended to be the basis of organizing what is observed by others. The Jordan Index summarizes the lifestyle of this person and indicates how disruptive this individual is likely to be in the workplace, in the classroom, and in personal relationships.

Managing Asperger's Syndrome

Getting along with Asperger's syndrome adults requires candid, clearly stated rules and guidelines. The social challenge of very high level autism includes limited recognition of social signals. These individuals do not recognize personal space boundaries, humor and friendly teasing, or abstract word usage. Adults with Asperger's syndrome think in literal, concrete images. They do not understand poetic language, puns, plays on word meanings, or double entendres (words with double meanings). Rules must be seen before they are understood fully.

Setting Limits

Those who work with, associate with, or live with Asperger's individuals must set limits. Failure to do so triggers resentment when privacy is invaded, irritation when personal space is crowded, and anger over habits of hair splitting and arguing. Limits must be stated visually and orally. The Asperger's individual must see a written statement of limits along with hearing them expressed orally. To get along with an Asperger's adult, others must make precise lists of what is unacceptable with enough detail to make the points absolutely clear. Adults with Asperger's syndrome cannot read between the lines or fill in implications that are not clearly expressed. Then these lists are clearly explained so the Asperger's person sees how something better can be put in the place of an inappropriate behavior. For example, a job supervisor or life partner might develop these rules:

1. When I hold up my hand with palm forward, it means that you need to back away and give me space.
2. When I speak your name firmly, it means that you must stop what you're doing (splitting, arguing, being disruptive, crowding too much).
3. When I ask you to look at our list of rules, you are not to argue with me.
4. When I pinch my nose and frown, it means that you forgot to wear a fresh shirt or change your socks.
5. When I point to my watch, it means that time is up and you are to leave me alone for half an hour.

Such frank rules of relationship may seem harsh, but this format of literal, concrete statements makes sense to a person with Asperger's syndrome. He or she may not like it, but this level of frankness leaves nothing to the imagination. Without expressing limits as written rules, it is impossible to work with, live with, or associate with Asperger's syndrome comfortably.

Changing Asperger's Behavior

Traditional psychotherapy does not change Asperger's behavior. Autism at whatever level of severity is caused by disconnect in brain pathways. Asperger's individuals cannot change how they process information or how they relate to the outside world. However, it is possible to modify Asperger's habits by substituting new rituals for old ones. It is not unusual for a lonely Asperger's person to ask: "Why don't people like me? Why don't they invite me when they do things together?" Such questions open the door for frank discussion. My response to these questions is to ask the Asperger's individual to write a list of times when he or she was not invited. With this list, we talk about each situation, pinpointing reasons why an invitation might not have been offered. As we talk this over, I ask candid questions: "Is it possible that you forgot to wear deodorant that week? Maybe you failed to wear fresh clothes?" Often this directness presents the Asperger's person with clear mental images that body odor is offensive and smelly clothes put others off.

This step-by-step analysis lets the Asperger's individual replace an undesirable ritual, such as wearing the same garment for five days without bathing, with a new ritual of bathing every morning and wearing fresh things. Over time, Asperger's individuals can learn to mimic acceptable social behaviors by memorizing them, as one memorizes any set of rules.

CHAPTER 4

Social-Emotional Learning Disability in Adults

DO CHILDREN OUTGROW LD?

Until the 1980s, most educators assumed that LD was a childhood issue. A few specialists in learning disabilities accepted the view of neuroscientists Albert Galaburda and Norman Geschwind that dyslexia is a lifelong learning disability (Galaburda, 1983; Geschwind, 1984). As attention deficit disorders, nonverbal LD, and social-emotional LD became the focus of research, much debate occurred about whether LD of whatever type is outgrown. By the early 1990s it was clear that approximately 80% of the early signs of LD begin to diminish as individuals pass through puberty (Barkley, 1995; Copeland, 1991; Denckla, 1993; Hallowell & Ratey, 1994a; Jordan, 1996a, 1996b, 1998; Weiss & Hechtman, 1993). Hormonal changes of puberty bring about late development along many brain pathways. By late teens, 80% of those who struggled hard with childhood LD patterns pass into a new level of learning ability. Remnants of childhood LD always will linger in adulthood, but 80% of LD youngsters outgrow enough LD symptoms to become successful adults. Unfortunately, 20% do not.

SOCIAL-EMOTIONAL LD IN ADULTHOOD

During the 20 years that nonverbal LD was studied and defined (1970–1990), research into disruptive behavior revealed a different type of social struggle that often shadows learning disabilities. As Chapter 3 described, nonverbal LD is caused by brain structural deficits in which links are missing between regions of the brain. This brain condition is called autism. Non-verbal LD is regarded as very high functioning autism. During the 1980s, a second type of nonacademic LD was named *Social-Emotional LD*, or SELD (Denckla, 1983; Duane, 1987; Osman & Blinder, 1982; Silver, 1985). This kind of disruptive behavior is linked to imbalances in the neurotransmitters dopamine, serotonin, norepinephrine, and acetylcholine (see Chapter 2). Autism and Nonverbal LD originate mostly in the wiring of the higher brain. Social-emotional disorders more often are linked to problems within the midbrain (limbic system).

SELD: SOCIAL-EMOTIONAL LD

Figure 4.1 shows the main regions of the midbrain (limbic system) that work together to regulate body chemistry, neurotransmitters, and brain enzymes that keep neurons firing in the right sequence and at the correct frequency. Chapter 2 described the main emotional centers of the brain (see Figure 2.4). When all is well within the brain, the prefrontal cortex stays in charge of behavior through logical reasoning and "social emotions" (patience, kindness, compassion, tolerance). Meanwhile, the limbic system cooperates by holding potentially destructive "antisocial emotions" in check (anger, jealousy, impulsivity, intolerance, fear, anxiety, depression).

One hundred years ago the British neuroscientist George Still described a type of disruptive lifestyle as "aggressive, defiantly resistant to discipline, emotionally volatile, lawless, spiteful, cruel, dishonest, and lacking in self-control" (Still, 1902, pp. 1008–1009). At the turn of the last century, such a candid report seemed unbelievable. By the 1980s, researchers had proved Still to be correct. Through brain imaging research, Martha Denckla, Bruce Pennington, Kytja Voeller, and others concluded that indeed our culture does include a disruptive population they described as *Social-Emotional LD* (Denckla, 1983, 1991a, 1991b, 1993; Pennington, 1991; Voeller, 1986, 1991). For example, Denckla's research found structural differences in the cerebellum that contribute to impulsivity, short attention, poor social skills, and inability to fit into the classroom, workplace, or society. To-

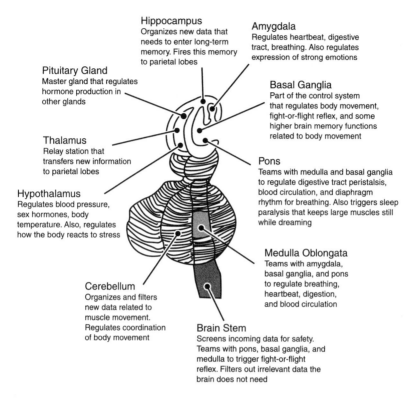

Hippocampus
Organizes new data that needs to enter long-term memory. Fires this memory to parietal lobes

Amygdala
Regulates heartbeat, digestive tract, breathing. Also regulates expression of strong emotions

Pituitary Gland
Master gland that regulates hormone production in other glands

Basal Ganglia
Part of the control system that regulates body movement, fight-or-flight reflex, and some higher brain memory functions related to body movement

Thalamus
Relay station that transfers new information to parietal lobes

Pons
Teams with medulla and basal ganglia to regulate digestive tract peristalsis, blood circulation, and diaphragm rhythm for breathing. Also triggers sleep paralysis that keeps large muscles still while dreaming

Hypothalamus
Regulates blood pressure, sex hormones, body temperature. Also, regulates how the body reacts to stress

Medulla Oblongata
Teams with amygdala, basal ganglia, and pons to regulate breathing, heartbeat, digestion, and blood circulation

Cerebellum
Organizes and filters new data related to muscle movement. Regulates coordination of body movement

Brain Stem
Screens incoming data for safety. Teams with pons, basal ganglia, and medulla to trigger fight-or-flight reflex. Filters out irrelevant data the brain does not need

Figure 4.1. All of these midbrain regions must work together as a well-coordinated team so that executive functions can work smoothly. If any of these members of the limbic system does not function well, an imbalance occurs in neurotransmitters and other brain enzymes. Such an imbalance allows strong emotions and disruptive behavior to take control over logical thinking and self-discipline.

day's adults with SELD are similar to the disruptive population described by Still a century ago.

EXECUTIVE FUNCTION

To understand Social-Emotional LD in adults, we must review the concept of *executive function* that was described in Chapter 2. When everything is well balanced within the brain, the prefrontal cortex and midbrain limbic system cooperate as a well-coordinated executive team. The brain functions like a highly organized community. The brain stem stands guard against threats to the community's safety. The midbrain and parietal lobes are receiving centers where incoming data is sorted and classified. The occipital lobes handle vision tasks. Temporal lobes do the listening, writing, and time keeping. Left and right sensory cortexes monitor odor, taste, and sensation to make sure the brain is not overloaded by too much strong stimulus. The motor cortexes make sure that muscle movement is balanced. Both frontal lobes oversee thinking, problem solving, and creativity. The executive in charge of all this community activity is the prefrontal cortex "upstairs" in the higher brain. The power station that regulates flow of energy, emotional surges, and the community alarm system is housed "downstairs" in the limbic system. Like all successful communities, brain activity must stay organized, correctly synchronized, well maintained though good health, and protected from threatening events. All of this is accomplished through collaboration between the executive function of the prefrontal cortex and the filtering, regulatory work of the limbic system.

The brain's executive function involves three major factors that work in harmony in most individuals: *organization, inhibition* (self-control), and *attention*. In fact, it is impossible to discuss intelligence, level of education, or individual talent if these executive function factors are out of balance. When midbrain regions are not doing their work properly, antisocial emotions are out of control. The person has very poor sense of organization. He or she has little self-control over impulses and sudden urges. There is little logical reasoning. This individual is continually in conflict with others. He or she does not live by the rules of society or accept responsibility for personal behavior. When executive function fails, disruptive behavior takes charge of the person's lifestyle. At some point, such irregular behavior is called Social-Emotional LD.

Appendix C presents the *Jordan Executive Function Inventory*. This questionnaire is designed to show the level of severity of SELD patterns in adults. Sometimes a disruptive person is mature enough to use this inventory as a self-evaluation activity. Sometimes an observer whom the individual trusts can do this inventory with the SELD person as a team activity. Usually a teacher, parent, or supervisor uses this questionnaire to pinpoint behaviors that disrupt life at home, in the workplace, or in the classroom.

OPPOSITIONAL DEFIANT BEHAVIOR: ODD SYNDROME

During the 1980s, Russell Barkley and his colleagues at the University of Massachusetts Medical Center mapped several types of disruptive behavior they found in the shadow of ADHD [Attention-Deficit Hyperactive Disorder] (Barkley, 1990). That research discovered that 65% of those diagnosed as ADHD also have a lifestyle of social-emotional LD called *Oppositional Defiant Disorder.* When attention deficits and hyperactivity are regulated through medication, these individuals usually become able to learn academic skills. However, 6 out of 10 ADHD individuals do not learn normal social behavior. Oppositional Defiant Disorder syndrome includes the following SELD behaviors:

1. Habitual temper tantrums for no apparent reason
2. Automatic arguing with authority figures
3. Deliberate defiance of rules and regulations
4. Automatic blaming of others instead of accepting personal responsibility
5. Being too touchy and too easily annoyed to tolerate normal social interaction
6. Being continually angry and resentful
7. Being continually spiteful and vindictive
8. Habitually cursing and using obscene language
9. Deliberately trying to annoy others

The impact of ODD upon others is easily seen. A person with ODD syndrome constantly is in conflict with others. This individual has no tolerance for the normal pressures and stresses of life. Relationships are clouded by outbursts of anger that explodes without warning. Others seldom see a connection between what is going on and a tantrum outburst from the ODD adult. Conversation is laced with strong language that often is obscene. When things are peaceful, this individual deliberately stirs up controversy just to have excitement. When he or she makes mistakes, there is automatic denial along with blaming someone else. Moments of affection are sabotaged by oversensitivity to imagined criticism. Adults with ODD feel sorry for themselves and go out of their way to play the role of martyr. Individuals with this lifestyle are extremely self-centered, thinking mostly of themselves while ignoring the needs or wishes of others. ODD persons rarely think positively. Virtually every thought is negative in some way. Not only do these individuals ignore rules and regulations, they choose to go against authority. Adults with ODD carry grudges with no intention ever to forgive. Their lives center around challenge of authority, rebellion, antagonism, aggressive self-defense, anger, and very short temper with no softening influence of higher motions such as gentleness, kindness, tolerance, or forgiveness. These persons are complainers who never find satisfaction. At work they are grumpy, at best. At worst, they are hostile and ill-tempered toward colleagues and supervisors. At home they lash out verbally at mates and children for no apparent reason. They inflict verbal and psychological abuse on others within their family circle. In society they heap abuse upon leaders, laws and regulations, and anyone who gets in the way.

CONDUCT DISORDER SYNDROME

Oppositional Defiant Disorder is at one end of a continuum of SELD behavior. Individuals with ODD syndrome are grouchy, angry, emotionally volatile, verbally abusive, and unpleasant. Yet they do not hurt others through physical attack. At the other end of the SELD disruptive behavior continuum is a lifestyle that often includes physical assault on people, living things, and property. This type of SELD is called *Conduct Disorder,* or CD syndrome. Barkley reports that 30% of those diagnosed as ADHD also have Conduct Disorder (Barkley, 1995). This aggressive, sometimes violent type of SELD is expressed through the following behaviors.

Aggression toward Animals and People

1. Bullying and intimidating people and animals who are helpless to defend themselves
2. Deliberately starting fights, usually over trivial issues
3. Threatening others with objects used as weapons (sticks, bats, rocks, metal objects, broken bottles, chains, knives, guns, or vehicles)
4. Life history of being physically cruel to animals and people
5. Life history of stealing from someone who is watching (mugging, purse snatching, blackmail extortion)
6. Life history of forcing others into unwanted sexual activity

Destruction of Property

1. Life history of setting fires to houses, buildings, forests, pasture land, trash dumps
2. Life history of vandalism toward homes, vehicles, public property, schools, businesses, personal property

Stealing and Lying

1. Life history of breaking into houses, businesses, schools, or public facilities in order to steal
2. Life history of stealing while no one is looking (shop lifting, pick-pocketing, taking things while visiting)
3. Life history of lying and denying that such crimes have been committed

Deliberate Violation of Rules

1. As a child or adolescent, ran way from home
2. As a child or adolescent, refused to obey curfews or other limits on personal freedom
3. Was often truant from school
4. History of traffic violations

Adults with Conduct Disorder inflict heavy trauma on families and society. These individuals often succeed in the workplace, but their attempts to be part of a family are chaotic. They inflict physical abuse on children, mates, and other relatives. Often they trigger dangerous conflict with neighbors. They display road rage attitudes in driving. They are bullies toward anyone who stands in their way. During childhood and early adolescence, persons with Conduct Disorder begin lifelong conflict with officers of the law. By adulthood, these aggressive, often violent individuals tend to serve prison time for assault, breaking and entering, robbery, murder, or attempted murder.

THE DYSLOGIC SYNDROME

Between the extremes of Oppositional Defiant Disorder (ODD) and Conduct Disorder (CD) is a third type of SELD that creates continual conflict. In the 1970s John Wacker published a monograph that described a disruptive lifestyle he called *The Dyslogic Syndrome* (Wacker, 1975). Later Keith Stanovich suggested that this type of SELD be called *Dysrationalia* (Stanovich, 1993). Individuals with this type of Social-Emotional LD often have advanced skills in reading, spelling, and writing. Often they obtain graduate degrees through high intelligence and good literacy skills. However, social skills and strong emotions are so out of balance that these individuals cannot fit into normal society. The following behaviors are found in the Dyslogic syndrome, or Dysrationalia.

1. Pays no attention to cause/effect. No thought of consequences
2. Displays very little rational/logical thinking or common sense reasoning
3. Lives by impulse
4. Is mostly self-focused
5. Makes aggressive, insatiable demands for instant wish fulfillment
6. Is insensitive to the needs and interests of others
7. Explodes in tantrums when challenged or denied

8. Makes irrational spur-of-the-moment decisions without regard to costly consequences
9. Cannot be relied upon or depended upon
10. Views the world through personal biases and prejudices. Lives by narrow values and interests of peer group
11. Does not learn from mistakes
12. Does not change habits because of moral or spiritual teaching
13. Is overly generous to members of peer group in irrational ways
14. Lives recklessly. Has no regard for risk to self
15. Seeks high-risk behavior. Achieves orgasmic-like emotional release through bringing self close to death or injury
16. Refuses to be responsible in traditional cultural sense
17. Lives an unconventional, nonconforming lifestyle
18. Is an irregular person in social behavior and lifestyle
19. Slavishly follows peer group fads
20. Is loyal only to the peer group or social group of the moment
21. Is ritualistic and obsessive about "dancing the tribal dance" of the moment
22. Is superstitious. Believes the myths, rumors, and half-truths told by peer group
23. Lives on gossip rather than fact
24. Thrives on rumor. Does not try to learn the truth
25. Is a shallow, superficial person living a shallow, superficial lifestyle
26. Has volatile emotions with rapid upsurges and downsurges of feelings
27. Is too sensitive to accept criticism. Cannot tolerate counseling or therapy
28. Usually is diagnosed ADHD, ODD, manic/depressive, character disordered, or borderline personality disorder type

LIFELONG SOCIAL-EMOTIONAL DISORDERS

These are the most frequent types of social-emotional disorders in adults in our society. These irregular lifestyles did not begin with adulthood. By studying youngsters in early childhood, we can identify behavior patterns that later will be recognized as

SELD, Oppositional Defiant Disorder, Conduct Disorder, and Dyslogic syndrome in adulthood. LD children who grow up to be LD adults bring much difficulty, struggle, conflict, and unhappiness across the border between adolescence and adulthood.

MANAGING SELD IN ADULTS

Social-emotional LD is caused by off-balance brain chemistry as well as cell structure differences in the midbrain. These biological factors make SELD an intensely personal issue. Our society does not always have legally sanctioned ways to keep explosive or dyslogical behavior under control. Regardless of disruptive differences, persons of legal age have the freedom to act as they choose, even when personal behavior disrupts life for others. Only when a disruptive person threatens his or her own life or the safety of others can society step in to place that individual under control.

Medication

Figure 4.2 summarizes the types of medications that are designed to reduce ADHD, ODD, CD, and dyslogical behavior in adults. Ironically, individuals with these types of Social-Emotional LD usually refuse to take medication that would change their behavior. A major factor in SELD is suspicion that borders on paranoia, the fear that others are "out to get me." Individuals 18 years or older cannot be forced to take behavior modification medication even when their conduct threatens to harm themselves or others. As Chapter 5 explains, these high-energy persons do not want to give up the emotional rush they experience in being aggressive. They choose to cling to destructive behavior rather than to become "normal."

Talking Therapy

Sometimes SELD adults want to talk with a sympathetic listener about their miseries and life struggles. When these windows

Cortical Stimulant for ADHD

Part of the short attention pattern in ADHD is lack of the neurotransmitter dopamine. Short supply of dopamine allows prefrontal cortex to "go to sleep" (underarousal) and lose control of executive function. Three medications are available to elevate levels of dopamine and arouse the prefrontal cortex to full executive alertness. It is important to use the lowest dosage possible so that the brain is not overmedicated.

Ritalin (methylphenidate) 5 to 15 mg daily; Nonaddictive and non-habit forming; 3% of adults cannot tolerate; Possible side effects: nausea, headache, nervousness, loss of appetite, trouble sleeping.

Cylert (pemoline) 35.5 mg; 3% of adults develop hepatitis symptoms; Possible side effects: skin rash or upset liver functions.

Dexedrine (dextroamphetamine) 5 to 15 mg; 3% of adults have unpleasant side effects like Ritalin.

Adderall 20 mg; A time-release version of Dexedrine.

Antiobsessive Medications

When the neurotransmitter serotonin is low, the midbrain loses control over strong, disruptive emotions and feelings. The midbrain cannot control impulses, the urge to repeat behaviors, or fretting/worrying. Obsessive, compulsive behavior can be reduced or stopped with medications that bring serotonin up to normal level. These medications are called SSRI (selective serotonin reuptake inhibitors).

Anafranil (clomitramine).

Prozac (fluoxetane).

Paxil (paraxetine).

Zoloft (certraline).

Luvox (fluoxamine maleate).

Effexor (vanlafaxine).

Serzone (nefazodone).

Sometimes an adult cannot tolerate an SSRI medication. If so, another SSRI usually is found to be comfortable.

Possible side effects are dry mouth, drowsiness, dizziness, or lethargy.

Antiagression Medications

When dopamine, serotonin, and acetylcholine are too high, the midbrain loses control over the impulse to be aggressive, have tantrums, behave violently, and rebel against authority. Several medications restore neurotransmitters to normal levels, which brings aggressive impulse under control of the prefrontal cortex executive function.

Catepres (clonodine).

Tenex (guanfacine).

Inderal (propanal hydrochloride).

Aurorix (moclobemide).

Possible side effects are drowsiness, lethargy, dry mouth, headache, dizziness, constipation, nausea, or stomachache.

Figure 4.2. These medications are effective in reducing or eliminating the symptoms of Social-Emotional LD. As with all medication, some individuals have allergic reactions (side effects) to some chemical compounds. With all of these medications, it is important to keep dosage to the lowest possible level for control of symptoms.

of opportunity open, it often is possible for a nonjudgmental listener to suggest ways by which the SELD individual can modify behavior in order to reduce stress and disappointment in their lives. Beneath the surface of aggressive, even bullying behavior often lie overly sensitive emotions and feelings. Those who disrupt society often are among the most sensitive individuals in the community. During my career I have seen hundreds of SELD adults ask for help. If they can find a listener whom they trust, these struggling individuals sometimes learn to change their most disruptive behaviors. It is amazing to see a tough-acting adult who exhibits road rage on the highway break into tears of regret over this aggressive behavior. During such moments of reflection, SELD individuals can examine their attitudes and habits deeply enough to learn how their behavior can be changed.

Diet Control

The controversial issue of how diet influences behavior remains unresolved. Two schools of thought continue to debate whether food and beverage intake contributes to learning difficulties or social misconduct. On one hand, the medical community generally believes that diet has little influence on learning, attention span, or behavior (Barkley, 1995; Barkley et al., 1991; Ingersoll & Goldstein, 1993). On the other hand, teachers and counselors often see direct connection between "trigger foods" and resulting explosive behavior (Bain, 1991; Conners, 1990; Green & Chee, 1994; Jordan, 1998; Warren & Capehart, 1995). Perhaps the reason these two points of view do not agree is lack of clarity between having a food allergy and being chemically intolerant of certain food elements. Certain persons are so highly allergic to specific food substances that they react as if they have been poisoned. This extreme allergic state is called *cytotoxic.* When a cytotoxic reaction to food or beverage occurs, the brain is attacked as if by poison. Brain tissues swell, axon pathways become inflamed, and neurotransmitters and other brain enzymes are thrown off balance. In that state, the brain stem and midbrain go on full alert, causing the prefrontal cortex to lose its executive, logical control. During this cytotoxic state, the individual is out of control over strong emotions and aggressive behavior.

A frequent trigger for intense hyperactivity and disruptive behavior is whole milk (Connors, 1990; Green & Chee, 1994; Jordan, 1998). Removing milk products from the diet often decreases or eliminates aggression, tantrums, or even violent behavior. Foods that contain ingredients made from grapes often trigger out-of-control reactions. Foods that contain salicylic acid tend to trigger aggressive behavior in some ADHD or SELD individuals. Eating or drinking such foods as strawberries, oranges, grapes, tomatoes, cucumber products, or bell peppers often sets off emotional explosions in persons who are cytotoxic to salicylic acid. Chemical dyes and preservatives that are added to foods and beverages often trigger aggression and tantrum behavior. Often it is possible to modify disruptive lifestyles by eliminating trigger foods and beverages.

CHAPTER 5

Emotional Shadows that Interfere with Learning and Remembering in Adults

During the Decade of the Brain, research into the causes of LD discovered a complex system of strong emotions and feelings that hide in the shadows of learning disabilities (Barkley et al., 1991, 1995; Damasio, 1994; Hallowell & Ratey, 1994a, 1994b; Jordan, 1996a, 1998; Ratey & Johnson, 1997; Schacter, 1996; Weiss & Hechtman, 1993). When adults do not outgrow childhood or adolescent learning difficulties, they bring an invisible burden of heavy emotions into adulthood. Often this undercurrent of negative feeling restricts their lives more than the learning disabilities.

Figure 5.1 presents the *Jordan Social-Emotional LD Mood Index* that maps the full range of emotions and feelings. At the low end of the mood index, suicidal thinking threatens the survival of deeply depressed individuals. At the high end of the mood index, out-of-control elation threatens life through accidental death. Within the workplace and continuing education are several million adults who suffer from manias and depression that hide in the shadows of lifelong struggle to learn.

DEPRESSION

In their book *Shadow Syndromes*, Ratey and Johnson (1997) describe the many ways in which depression sabotages the lives of adults, especially those who are LD. In *Attention Deficit Disorder: ADHD and ADD Syndromes*, I describe forms of depression that usually accompany ADD (Jordan, 1998). In their popular books *Answers to Distraction* and *Driven to Distraction*, Hallowell and Ratey (1994a, 1994b) explore the impact of de-

JORDAN SOCIAL-EMOTIONAL LD MOOD INDEX

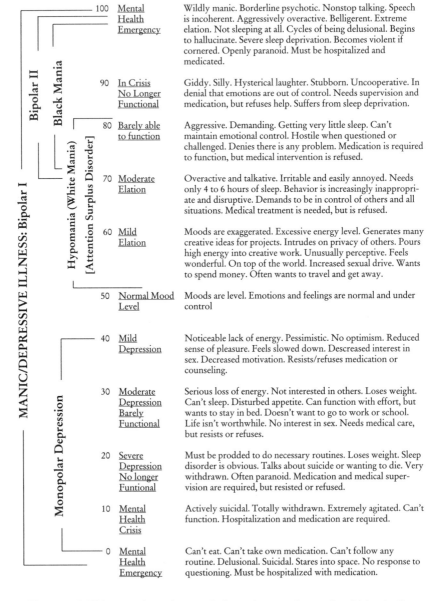

100	Mental Health Emergency	Wildly manic. Borderline psychotic. Nonstop talking. Speech is incoherent. Aggressively overactive. Belligerent. Extreme elation. Not sleeping at all. Cycles of being delusional. Begins to hallucinate. Severe sleep deprivation. Becomes violent if cornered. Openly paranoid. Must be hospitalized and medicated.
90	In Crisis No Longer Functional	Giddy. Silly. Hysterical laughter. Stubborn. Uncooperative. In denial that emotions are out of control. Needs supervision and medication, but refuses help. Suffers from sleep deprivation.
80	Barely able to function	Aggressive. Demanding. Getting very little sleep. Can't maintain emotional control. Hostile when questioned or challenged. Denies there is any problem. Medication is required to function, but medical intervention is refused.
70	Moderate Elation	Overactive and talkative. Irritable and easily annoyed. Needs only 4 to 6 hours of sleep. Behavior is increasingly inappropriate and disruptive. Demands to be in control of others and all situations. Medical treatment is needed, but is refused.
60	Mild Elation	Moods are exaggerated. Excessive energy level. Generates many creative ideas for projects. Intrudes on privacy of others. Pours high energy into creative work. Unusually perceptive. Feels wonderful. On top of the world. Increased sexual drive. Wants to spend money. Often wants to travel and get away.
50	Normal Mood Level	Moods are level. Emotions and feelings are normal and under control
40	Mild Depression	Noticeable lack of energy. Pessimistic. No optimism. Reduced sense of pleasure. Feels slowed down. Decreased interest in sex. Decreased motivation. Resists/refuses medication or counseling.
30	Moderate Depression Barely Functional	Serious loss of energy. Not interested in others. Loses weight. Can't sleep. Disturbed appetite. Can function with effort, but wants to stay in bed. Doesn't want to go to work or school. Life isn't worthwhile. No interest in sex. Needs medical care, but resists or refuses.
20	Severe Depression No longer Funtional	Must be prodded to do necessary routines. Loses weight. Sleep disorder is obvious. Talks about suicide or wanting to die. Very withdrawn. Often paranoid. Medication and medical supervision are required, but resisted or refused.
10	Mental Health Crisis	Actively suicidal. Totally withdrawn. Extremely agitated. Can't function. Hospitalization and medication are required.
0	Mental Health Emergency	Can't eat. Can't take own medication. Can't follow any routine. Delusional. Suicidal. Stares into space. No response to questioning. Must be hospitalized with medication.

MANIC/DEPRESSIVE ILLNESS: Bipolar I

Bipolar II

Black Mania

Hypomania (White Mania) [Attention Surplus Disorder]

Monopolar Depression

Figure 5.1. This complex mixture of disruptive emotions often hides in the shadow of LD, NVLD, and SELD adolescents and adults. Based upon research reported by the Menninger Foundation in Topeka, Kansas.

pression in adolescents and adults with attention deficit disorders. My book *Overcoming Dyslexia in Children, Adolescents, and Adults* documents the heavy burden of depression in adults who are dyslexic (Jordan, 1996a).

WHAT IS DEPRESSION?

Depression is defined generally as "anger turned inward." When a person feels the first moments of stress, the brain stem signals the possibility of emotional danger. Chapter 2 describes the fight-or-flight reflex (see Figure 2.4) that regulates how the brain copes with episodes of stress. When all is well and individuals feel self-confident, a surge of courage prepares the brain to fight by getting busy resolving problems that trigger stress. However, when all is not well and self-confidence is low, the brain often chooses not to fight but to flee into emotional safety. Figure 5.2 shows the brain regions that govern how a person responds to stress. Too much stress triggers the decision not to fight but to hide from whatever is threatening one's well-being. When stress comes from such sources as job failure, personal loss, school failure, financial loss, sleep deprivation, illness, shame, or extreme guilt, the brain may suppress normal anger by denying that a threatening situation exists. This denial of reality starts the brain chemistry process that turns anger inward where it is locked inside instead of turning outward to resolve problems.

Situational Depression

Most individuals go through times of being depressed for a while. Situational depression is caused by a type of emotional shock that triggers temporary brain chemistry imbalance. Unexpected financial loss, critical illness of a loved one, lack of sleep for stressful reasons, shame, guilt, losing one's job, a breakdown in a personal relationship confront individuals with more stress than they can tolerate. For LD individuals who struggle to learn, pressures encountered in the classroom commonly trigger depression. As problems are resolved and situations improve, brain

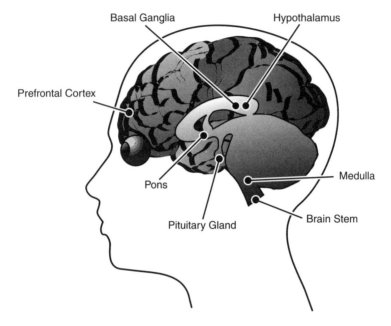

Figure 5.2. Stress from threatening events, such as illness, personal loss, overwhelming responsibilities, shame, failure, sleep deprivation, or intolerable social pressure triggers the fight-or-flight reflex that is regulated by the pons, basal ganglia, and medulla. If the brain decides to fight, the person becomes angry enough to take a stand and resolve threatening issues. If the brain decides not to fight, then emotions and feelings "take flight" by suppressing anger and denying that it exists. This suppressed anger turns into depression. At the first moment of stress, the hypothalamus takes charge of hormone production. The hypothalamus signals the pituitary gland and other members of the body chemistry system to change the balance of neurotransmitters and brain enzymes. This altered state of body chemistry energizes the brain to fight for safety, or it commands the midbrain to guard emotions and feelings through a state of depression.

chemistry comes back into normal balance and the cloud of depression lifts or goes away. A common type of situational depression is *Seasonal Affective Disorder* (SAD) that afflicts millions of individuals during winter months of prolonged lack of sunlight. Depression often is triggered by invisible changes in health, such as low thyroid, hypoglycemia, anemia, Type II diabetes, or hormone reduction during menopause and aging. Situational depression is especially common in persons with learning disabilities. Making good grades often eliminates depression for a while. Failure to continue making good grades brings back the heaviness of depression that is linked to poor classroom performance.

Monopolar Depression

Figure 5.1 describes a type of permanent depression that does not change with time or circumstance. Individuals with monopolar depression never rise above the state of being mildly depressed. Sometimes this condition of chronic sadness lasts a lifetime. As with other forms of depression, this constant state of inner darkness is caused by too little serotonin in the brain. Monopolar depression rises and falls without ever breaking through the ceiling into normal or elated feelings. Persons with this deep state of depression feel a tightness in the chest, like a hand squeezing the heart. Monopolar depression feels like intense grief that catches one's breath and enfolds one's heart in heaviness almost too intense to bear. Ironically, individuals with this mood disorder seldom cry. As they describe their emotional anguish, they talk of despair that is too deep for tears. Many adults who are trapped in this cavern of sadness speak of spiritual darkness that fills them with dread and nightmares of tragedies to come. Yet tears rarely flow in this deep state of dejection.

Monopolar depression numbs the higher brain functions like an anesthetic. The person is awake, yet higher brain regions seem to be asleep. Often it is difficult, sometimes impossible, for these individuals to function at work, at school, or at home. Knowledge and experience are beyond their reach behind the heavy veil of grief that never ends and which seldom has an obvious cause. Living year after year with monopolar depression is an invisible struggle that brings undeserved criticism and condemnation: "Oh, get hold of yourself! Everyone has problems. You just don't try hard enough to cheer up. I'm tired of seeing you mope around all the time." These angry criticisms from job supervisors, instructors, friends, and loved ones make the emotional fog of depression even heavier. Monopolar depression is not caused by failing to try harder. It is caused by dysfunctions in brain chemistry that are far beyond the control of those who suffer from this type of depression.

Depression with LD

During the Decade of the Brain, much attention was directed to the overlap of depression and different types of learning disability (Alexander-Roberts, 1995; Barkley, 1995; Hallowell & Ratey, 1994a; Jordan, 1996a, 1998; Ratey & Johnson, 1997; Weiss & Hechtman, 1993). Adolescents and adults with dyslexia, ADHD or ADD, Oppositional Defiant Disorder (ODD), nonverbal LD, Social-Emotional LD, and Scotopic Sensitivity syndrome are at much higher risk for depression than individuals with no LD. Depression in these LD persons often is situational. As problems are resolved, lifestyle improves, job or school performance rises, or personal relationships become more positive, depression tends to lift for a while. But when new events occur that threaten emotional safety, LD individuals tend to plunge back into states of depression that engulf them in anxiety, fear, and sadness. In states of severe depression, adolescents and adults who are LD frequently ponder suicide, even planning how they might destroy themselves to escape their miseries. We do not know how many severely depressed LD individuals attempt or succeed at suicide. However, we who counsel LD individuals hear many confessions of suicidal thinking and wishing for death. In *Overcoming Dyslexia in Children, Adolescents, and Adults,* I present numerous biographical accounts of adults who have learned to succeed in spite of dyslexia (Jordan, 1996a). Depression and thoughts of dying are common themes as LD adolescents and adults tell their life stories. States of depression create all kinds of heartache and failure for persons who are LD, such as job failure, loss of personal relationships, shattered self-esteem and self-confidence, school failure, humiliation, shame, and periods of grief too heavy for words to express.

Anxiety with Depression

For many LD adults, depression is wrapped inside a painful emotional cover of constant anxiety. Symptoms of depression are active: sadness, withdrawal, turning feelings inward, dreading each new day, emotional fatigue, refusing intimacy, and so forth. In addition to these heavy emotions is a state of anxiety that drives the person to the edge of tolerance through fretting, worrying, and overreacting to anything new or different. When depression is overlapped by anxiety, the individual is the victim of nonstop fear. "What was that? What if I get the flu and can't work? What do you mean by that? I won't go because I know they don't want to be around me. What if my paycheck is late? What if I can't pay the bills this month? I'm not going to drive to see your folks. What if we have a flat after dark, or the car breaks down?" These kinds of anxious questions torment the person day and night. If medication is recommended to ease anxiety and relieve depression, a form of paranoia emerges. "What if the medication doesn't work? What if it makes me worse? What if I have a bad reaction? It scares me to think of taking pills every day." If counseling is suggested as a way of talking through these negative feelings, resistance springs to life. "Are you saying I'm crazy? What would a counselor do except charge me money? I've heard that you can't trust counselors to keep your talks secret." Living with a person whose depression is wrapped inside anxiety can become intolerable. This constant dark fretting and worrying drain away the strength of those who share the same space. It is impossible to talk with the troubled individual about these issues without triggering arguments and self-pitying outbursts. Yet to be silent sets off cascades of complaints: "Why don't you ever talk to me? What's wrong with me that you aren't telling me? Why do you act like you're mad at me all the time? You just don't understand what I'm going through!" Depression overlapped by anxiety takes the LD individual beyond the reach of normal affection and concern.

MANIA

Depression often is linked with an opposite emotional state called mania, or manic behavior. In their book *Shadow Syn-*

dromes, Ratey and Johnson describe the "noisy brain" that never hushes. Day and night, the manic brain churns with thoughts and mental images that disrupt normal brain activity (Ratey & Johnson, 1997). The noisy brain cannot maintain internal communication, as Chapter 2 describes. Mania is the state of nonstop "brain chatter" that cannot be still. When mania is linked to depression, the individual's emotions and feelings are made more intense by chronic anxiety that never lets the brain rest from obsessive worry and fretting. Frequently depression is wrapped inside frantic episodes of panic disorder, an extreme manic state that includes phobic-level fears. As LD adults age, these underlying emotional states tend to increase, even for individuals who achieve success.

MANIC/DEPRESSIVE ILLNESS: BIPOLAR I

Manic/Depressive Illness, also called *Bipolar I,* is an emotional roller coaster that drives feelings and emotions up and down the mood index. Manic/Depressive Illness: Bipolar I is caused by imbalance in neurotransmitters and other brain enzymes. This body chemistry imbalance releases potentially destructive emotions and feelings that are too strong to remain under control of the prefrontal cortex. Some individuals have wide mood swings several times a day. Again and again within 24 hours they spiral upward into the range of elation and giddy happiness, then drop into the darkness of sadness and depression. With other persons, mood shifts up and down the index are very slow, taking several months to pass from depression to elation, then back to depression. Bipolar I Manic/Depressive Illness creates emotional instability that leaves the individual unable to think clearly, maintain motivation, follow through on plans and goals, and perform competently. Those who suffer from Manic/Depressive Illness cannot be relied upon to meet schedules or do good work on the job or in the classroom. Yet this social-emotional deficit may hide in the shadows for many years without being recognized or diagnosed.

HYPOMANIA

White Mania

In her autobiography *An Unquiet Mind,* Kay Jamison (1995) tells the electrifying story of her years of unrelieved mania that hurled her up and down the mood swings of Bipolar I (mania and depression) and Bipolar II (black mania). Occasionally Jamison's noisy brain calmed down to the level of mild elation (level 60), as Figure 5.1 describes. Sometimes her emotions and feelings dropped into the dark cavern of depression (level 30 or 20). Mostly her manic state was above level 70 on the index. Jamison describes how SELD individuals can live for years at a moderately manic level called *hypomania.*

> I simply did not want to believe that I needed to take medication. I had become addicted to my high moods; I had become dependent upon their intensity, euphoria, assuredness, and their infectious ability to induce high moods and enthusiasms in other people ... I found my milder manic states powerfully inebriating and very conducive to productivity. I couldn't give them up. (pp. 98–99)

This state of elation can be highly productive as creative ideas flow from the overly aroused "noisy brain" that never stops talking to itself, even during sleep (Jamison, 1995; Jordan, 1998; Ratey & Johnson, 1997). In spite of continual flow of new ideas, individuals with hypomania often fail to succeed unless others turn these ideas into reality. Hypomania is too loose and too poorly organized to follow through to completion. Adults with hypomania bombard their environments with Social-Emotional LD behaviors that "drive others to distraction," as Hallowell and Ratey have described. Often it is impossible for hypomanic persons to manage a business, hold a marriage together, stay in school, or maintain good relationships with children and other relatives. Hypomania is so disruptive that others look for ways to avoid or get away from these aggressive individuals. Persons with hypomania are bullies, demanding to be in control of everyone and everything in their lives. They develop complex systems of control techniques that range from weeping in order to wear others down through guilt to furious tantrums that force others to agree just to have peace. As a child in rural Oklahoma, I learned the meaning of a bit of local wisdom: "A dog can lick a skunk, but it ain't worth it." Those who must deal with hypomanic persons give in rather than fight. Winning a battle of wits with hypomania is not worth the emotional price one must pay to do so.

LD and Hypomania

Many adolescents and adults who have LD also have cycles of elation and depression (Jordan, 1998). Individuals with ADHD (attention deficit with hyperactivity) display habits that are similar to hypomania (Barkley, 1995; Ratey & Johnson, 1997). Both hypomania and ADHD involve a short attention span. In ADHD, attention can stay focused on certain types of activity for prolonged periods of time. It is impossible for the hypomanic person to stay mentally focused in any event. No matter how hard the manic individual tries, he or she cannot keep from jumping track and darting off on different mental activities. ADHD individuals do not necessarily try to stay in control of others and events. Hypomanic persons always do. ADHD does not rise and fall in intensity. Hypomania cannot stay the same. ADHD usually includes low self-esteem and low self-confidence. Hypomania struts and brags from exaggerated self-importance. The following cluster of behaviors differentiate hypomania from ADHD:

1. Exaggerated self-esteem. Attitude of grandiosity
2. Reduced need for sleep
3. Nonstop talking
4. Racing thoughts and mental images
5. Distractibility in all situations
6. Fixated attention on goal-directed activities. Must develop a plan for every situation
7. Compulsion for high-pleasure activities, regardless of cost or consequences

Attention Surplus Disorder

Another name for hypomania is *Attention Surplus Disorder.* This manic mental state generates so much inner noise that the brain lives in a condition of chronic confusion and emotional frustration. The following behaviors are symptoms of Attention Surplus Disorder:

1. Hyperactive development of thoughts and mental images
2. Constant jumping from one incomplete thought to another
3. Rapid speech that leaves out syllables and grammar chunks
4. Sense of being frantic to tell what the person is thinking
5. Inability to speak fast enough to keep up with racing thoughts
6. Questions that tumble out in rapid sequence, but person cannot listen to answers
7. Becomes overly frustrated and irritable when others interrupt the torrents of spoken thoughts
8. Places great stress on others through hyperactive speech and escalating irritability
9. Cannot participate in normal slower rhythms of social conversation
10. Creates conflict by challenging, contradicting, and arguing over what was said or not said
11. Creates dread in others of having conversations or personal encounters with this emotionally driven, hyperactive thinker

BIPOLAR II: BLACK MANIA

The upper end of the mood index is called *Bipolar II: Black Mania* because of the severity of out-of-control emotions and feelings. Again, Jamison (1995) describes the horrid mental state of black mania:

> Both my manias and depression had violent sides to them. . . . Being wildly out of control—physically assaultive, screaming insanely at the top of (my) lungs, running frequently with no purpose or limit, or impulsively trying to leap from (moving) cars. . . . I have, in my black, agitated manias destroyed things I cherish, pushed to the utter edge people I love, and survived to think I could never recover from the shame. . . . (p. 120)

The possibility of accidental suicide is a major concern for individuals who are in a state of black mania. As Jamison described, she had irrational impulses to leap from moving vehicles. Numerous adolescents and adults I have counseled have described finding themselves atop high water towers or on rooftops about to jump. They were not trying to die. In their delusional Bipolar II state, they imagined that they could fly or "leap to the moon." Many high-speed, single-vehicle accidents occur when the driver is in a delusional black mania state. The driver imagines that the vehicle can fly over an approaching river, leap over a looming highway overpass, or pass under the bed of a truck.

The traffic problem of road rage often involves Bipolar II delusions. Recently a near-fatal road rage episode exploded on a highway near our home. An enormous truck-and-trailer rig was hauling coils of rolled steel, each of which weighed 20 tons. A smaller vehicle passed the large rig, then moved into the right lane ahead of the truck. This legal act by the second driver triggered rage in the trucker's brain. Later he explained that he imagined the small vehicle driver had yelled insults as he "cut me off" in traffic. In his black mania state, the trucker decided to punish the smaller vehicle by running over it. The driver of the huge rig accelerated to 100 miles per hour and chased the second vehicle down the highway. Horrified drivers pulled onto the shoulder as the enraged trucker pursued the offending driver. Finally the truck crashed into an overpass bridge rail, which stopped the chase. A 20-ton coil of steel fell onto the overpass, destroying the roadway in that lane. Later it was learned that the trucker was under the influence of stimulants to keep him awake. He also reported that he is dyslexic and always has trouble knowing left from right. He had no memory of driving 100 miles per hour or of swerving into the wrong lane of the highway.

LD AND MANIC/DEPRESSIVE ILLNESS

Perhaps specific learning disabilities and manic/depression are related syndromes. During the Decade of the Brain, Barkley estimated that 45% of individuals who are ADHD also have Bipolar I Manic/Depressive Illness (Barkley, 1995). Types of LD and variations of manic/depression often are passed down family genetic lines. Both syndromes are linked to specific chromosomes and gene markers. LD and manic/depressive disorders manifest lifelong patterns of make-believe and fantastical thinking. Difficulty paying full attention is seen in mood disorders and learning disabilities. Long-term memory is spotty and incomplete in LD and manic/depression. Poor performance in the classroom, on the job, and in family relationships exists in both syndromes. Except for the delusional self-importance of hypomania, both manic/depression and LD foster low self-esteem and very low self-confidence. The risk of self-destruction through suicide exists in both syndromes. Because of these biological and behavioral links between LD and manic/depression, it is all the more important that mood disorders, which often hide in the shadows of learning difficulties, be recognized and treated.

Managing Manic/Depressive Emotions and Feelings

In his book *Violence,* James Gilligan (1996), a psychiatrist who specializes in violence within prison systems, presents his concepts of changing out-of-control emotions, feelings, and behaviors:

> I am convinced that violent behavior, even at its most apparently senseless, incomprehensible, and psychotic, is an understandable response to an identifiable, specifiable set of conditions; and that even when it seems motivated by "rational" self-interest, it is the end product of a series of irrational, self-destructive, and unconscious motives that can be studied, identified, and understood. (p. 102)

Talking Therapy

The foundation of Gilligan's therapy is the concept that shame drives most of the self-destructive behavior in our society. As Jamison acknowledged, her self-destructive lifestyle left her with incredible shame. In *Overcoming Dyslexia in Children, Adolescents, and Adults,* I discuss the powerful role of shame in individuals who are dyslexic. Perhaps the most commonly heard self-description from LD individuals is: "I'm dumb. I'm too stupid to learn how to do that." Releasing struggling learners from their sense of shame over "being dumb" is a dramatic experience in becoming emotionally free from old bondage. "You mean I'm not dumb? I always thought I was too dumb. Now I know I'm not dumb. I just have a learning problem." This jubilant cry comes from countless LD persons who understand for the first time that they need not feel shame for having a learning disability.

Talking therapy is a powerful source of healing as we help manic or depressive individuals learn to deal with mood swings, old emotions, and lifelong feelings. As mental health therapists like Gilligan have demonstrated, it is possible to replace hopeless shame with hopeful self-understanding that conquers shame. This process is much like a spiritual awakening that allows hopeless individuals to see beyond themselves. Being set free from shame, humiliation, and low self-esteem opens new opportunities that LD adults may never before have seen. Talking through emotional issues with a listener who understands without judgment breaks open the emotional cage where shameful attitudes have been locked for a lifetime.

Knowledge of Self

Often the most liberating experience an LD or manic/depressive person can have is to gain information and knowledge about oneself. Countless times during my career I have shared frank information with strugglers who had no idea why they struggled to learn, why they remained so depressed, why their moods swung up and down out of control, or why they suffered intensely from guilt and shame. The Decade of the Brain has provided fascinating new information about how the brain learns and remembers, along with new data about what causes LD. As adults with learning difficulties learn about LD in their family lines, they are set free from believing they are alone in their struggles. As these individuals learn about the critical role our emotions and feelings play, adults realize for the first time why they have phobic memories of school situations that keep them from success in adult education. Learning facts about the role of neurotransmitters in mental health washes away self-blame for being different. Discovering through diagnostic testing that they are bright, not "dumb," melts clouds of low self-esteem from the emotional landscape. "I'm not dumb!" becomes a mantra that plants new hope in place of despair.

Countless times I have witnessed sudden transformation in self-confidence when a deeply depressed individual learned the truth about his or her intelligence. This radiant freedom from despair was made crystal clear one afternoon following an evaluation and family conference in my office. That 14-year-old boy had come to me that morning in a state of such depression he could not look me in the face or communicate above a mumble. After becoming comfortable enough with me to know that he was safe, he agreed to do an intelligence test. The results were electrifying: Verbal IQ 124, Performance IQ 132, Full Scale IQ 130. I showed him a chart that ranked this intelligence at the 97th percentile. "You are more intelligent than 97 out of 100 other kids your age," I explained. In an explosion of joy, that information released the boy from depression by giving him new hope. All the way to the parking lot he shouted: "Mom, I'm not dumb! I'm not stupid! Mom, I'm not dumb!" With tutoring to strengthen reading and writing skills, that dyslexic young man graduated from high school and college with honors and became a licensed psychological counselor. Not surprisingly, he is building a career helping struggling learners overcome LD.

A life-changing release surprised a young adult who came to me at his mother's insistence. At age 21, Clayton was a school failure, could not hold a job, and was unable to develop lasting romantic relationships. On the surface, this man appeared self-assured and confident. He was tall, handsome, and well groomed. As we worked through a series of diagnostic activities, I began to see barely concealed anxiety toward spelling and reading. When Clayton broke into heavy perspiration from inner stress, I suggested that we take a break. I also turned off bright lights, leaving my office in a soft indirect glow from a lamp. Later I discovered that Clayton had moderately severe Scotopic Sensitivity syndrome that is described in Chapter 1. In telling me about himself, he described his father's early death when Clayton was two years old. The parents were in their late teens and had not had a formal wedding. His father dropped out of school to support his wife and child. There were no wedding or graduation pictures for the son to treasure. The only picture Clayton had of his dad was a faded snapshot that showed a young man who closely resembled Clayton. "I tried to go to college," he said quietly. "But my high school grades were too low for me to get a scholarship." Without warning, his eyes filled with tears. He clenched his teeth to keep from sobbing as he gripped his chair with white knuckles. Clayton bowed his head to cut off eye contact. On a hunch, I said: "Clayton, is it possible that you are having some problems with shame?"

This struggling young man exploded into deep sobs. Obviously he was in serious emotional pain. Through his tears he gasped: "I'm no good. I can't do anything right. I'm nothing but a cheat. My daddy would be so ashamed of me!" Then his sobs became too intense for him to talk. Finally he said: " I miss my daddy so much! But I know he would be ashamed of me if he were still here."

In my work with struggling adolescents and adults, often I add touching or holding to exploratory talking that triggers deep emotions. I knelt beside Clayton's chair and put my arms around his shoulders. Suddenly he turned and grasped me in a crushing embrace. He buried his face on my shoulder and continued to sob for several minutes. "I miss my daddy so much!" he repeated. "I've dreamed so many times about him holding me like this. I've dreamed about what it would be like to hug my daddy and have him hug me." Then Clayton straightened and turned me loose. "But he would be too ashamed of me. I can't read. I can't spell or write. I've cheated to get through school. I'm nothing but a fake and a cheat. My daddy would be so ashamed of me."

This intense emotional release brought Clayton back to a level state of feeling. As we finished the evaluation, I was frank in showing him his test results and explaining what I discovered in his learning patterns. He was fascinated to know that he was dyslexic, which I explained by showing him the dyslexic patterns presented in Chapter 1. For the first time, he understood why he could never learn to spell, sound out words, or write correctly. He could not believe the dramatic way in which color overlays, in his case two layers of purple, stopped print distortions, as shown in Chapter 1. With the print stabilized and clear, he began to read, and read, and read. Clayton began to cry again, but this time he shed tears of joy. As we finished our work, his sense of shame was replaced by joy. "I can't believe what you've done for me," he said several times. "I'm not dumb! I'm dyslexic, and I'm Scotopic. But I'm not dumb!" he marveled. Then he asked: "Is it possible my daddy was dyslexic? Do you think that's why he dropped out of school?" We discussed the likelihood that his father might have been dyslexic. For the first time, Clayton had a tangible link with the dad he loved so deeply.

Not all struggling adults find relief so quickly. However, it is not unusual for new self-knowledge to bring rapid emotional freedom to adults like Clayton. As Gilligan has shown, strongly antisocial behavior often turns around quickly when talking therapy is frank, honest, and straightforward. When shame is replaced by clear data that explains lifelong difficulty, adults like Clayton do not need prolonged therapy to develop a new self-image based upon hope and success.

Medication

In Chapter 4, Figure 4.2 describes the range of medications that reduce or eliminate distraction, obsessive behaviors, and aggression. Before the Decade of the Brain, the most commonly used medication for Manic/Depressive Illness or monopolar depression was lithium. Today a wider range of antidepression medications is available. For depression, the most commonly used medications are *Aventyl* and *Pamelor* (forms of nortriptyline), *Petrofrane* and *Norpramin* (forms of desipramine), *Welbutrin* (buproprion hydrochloride), *BuSpar* (buspirone), *Tofranil* (imipramine), *Tryptonal* (amitryptilline), and *Elavil* (amitriptyline). For manic/depressive or obsessive/compulsive behavior, the SSRI medications shown in Figure 4.2 are the most frequently used.

CHAPTER 6

Learning Disabilities and Aging

Chapter 4 describes how 80% of LD youngsters outgrow enough symptoms to succeed in higher education or workplace skill training. As these young adults finish maturing during their 20s and early 30s, residual LD patterns continue to decline (Jordan, 1996b. 1998). By age 40 few of these "late bloomers" still need accommodation for LD. In contrast are the 20% of adults who do not outgrow childhood LD. They always need accommodation and assistance to get by in life. Because LD patterns travel down family DNA lines, diagnosticians frequently hear parents say: "I was like that when I was a child. No one ever explained why I had such a hard time in school. Will my son (or daughter) outgrow it like I did?" Until adults who have outgrown LD are confronted by such memories, they tend to forget that their early years were frustrated by learning problems.

A PERSONAL PERSPECTIVE

Writing this book has been an emotional autobiographical experience for me. As a child 60-some years ago, I struggled with every kind of school performance except public speaking. Verbal expression was a special talent that brought praise and honor through winning speech competitions. Yet in the classroom, I was miserable. I was dyslexic in handwriting, ADD in paying attention, unable to grasp higher math concepts, hyperactive and impulsive in social behavior, and prone to bouts of depression I never revealed to anyone. As I proudly added speech tournament trophies to the school display case, my self-esteem remained very low, and I had no self-confidence outside those moments of glib speaking. I finished high school with grade average just above failing. How could my teachers fail the student who had won a national 4-H Club championship, along with several state and regional debate tournaments?

My first attempt at college was as miserable as public school had been, ending with grade average of 1.3. This lifelong academic struggle convinced me that I was not fit for college studies. Then about age 23 an astonishing thing happened. I found myself reading voraciously in heavy literature that was beyond my ability at age 20. My mind began to hunger for formal knowledge. A merciful university agreed to let me try again on probation. This time my grade average was 3.8, and my doctorate was finished with honors. By age 36 my formerly noisy LD brain was filled by a new kind of sound, that of nonstop creativity pouring out as published work that would have been impossible 10 years earlier. Aging, I decided, was the answer to youth's problems.

When I reached age 55, a mysterious thing began to happen. Gradually I became LD again. Letter and number reversals appeared increasingly often in my spelling and math computation, while handwriting deteriorated to my school-days scrawl. Tracking what I heard (auditory perception) required much more effort. Words began to change on the page, as they had when I was young. Without warning during reading, *Tulsa* flipped to Altus. *Reverse* changed to reserve. Continually I read *sliver* for silver. Sustained reading became so filled with these visual dyslexic blips that I had to back up and read everything again, just to be sure. This reemergence of LD has continued, and I am sure that it will not diminish in the decades ahead. Aging, I have discovered, is only temporarily the answer for youth's problems. Whatever LD symptoms we put aside as we enter adulthood return as we pass into early old age.

BRAIN CHANGES IN AGING

The Decade of the Brain revealed much new information about changes that occur in the brain, starting in most adults about age 55 (Atchley, 1994; Birren, Sloane, & Cohen, 1992; Charness & Bosman, 1992; Fisher, 1992; Hooker, 1992; Kogan, 1990; Lee & Cerami, 1990; Park, 1992; Raskin & Peskind, 1992; Schieber, 1992). Ironically, language and thought processing behaviors linked to these middle-age changes in brain structure are very similar to the LD behaviors diagnosed in children. Recently I saw a vivid forecast of what my own LD patterns might become if I survive into advanced old age. My mother, now 93 years old and still living alone, always has been an avid jigsaw puzzle worker. A table in her home always has a puzzle in progress. All my life I have been fascinated by her quickness in left-to-right, top-to-bottom spatial relationships that show her which pieces fit which spaces. As I entered her home on a recent visit, I stopped in amazement. The half-assembled puzzle on her table was upside down. Her aging brain had developed mirror image that perceives objects upside down and backward. She was unaware that this "LD shift" had occurred. This experience helped our family understand many things about my mother's aging behavior. Her brain is no longer fluent in interpreting her world left-to-right and top-to-bottom. She struggles to add or subtract in keeping her checkbook. Her penmanship is becoming dysgraphic. Yet her mind is clear and active in long-term memory and keeping track of current events. In telling, she loses her words, but her thought content is intact and intelligent.

As we age, many of us develop "glitches" in thought processing that increasingly resemble childhood patterns we call LD:

1. Needing extra time
2. Failing to respond to normal levels of verbal stimulus
3. Being uncertain in making decisions
4. Needing to hear new information again
5. Making many more mistakes when pressed to hurry
6. Holding back from starting tasks until procedures are clear
7. Feeling anxious about failing and making mistakes
8. Reviewing finished work several times before being satisfied that it is correct
9. Needing second chances to do tasks correctly
10. Veering off track instead of staying on task
11. Feeling unsure or uneasy about choices and decisions
12. Forgetting to finish what is started
13. Misplacing or losing things
14. Being slow to comprehend the full meaning of new information

15. Dreading or resisting changes in familiar routines
16. Making mistakes in comprehension while listening and reading

CHANGES IN EXECUTIVE FUNCTION

Chapter 2 describes executive function, which is how the prefrontal cortex stays in charge of brain functions. As most children mature, executive function becomes well organized and able to meet the demands of one's lifestyle. The Decade of the Brain revealed that executive function undergoes important changes during middle age. In our mid-50s these changes are subtle and easily ignored. As individuals enter "younger old age" of their 60s, changes in executive function become more noticeable and pronounced. Adults who outgrew early learning difficulties find forgotten LD symptoms reappearing in spelling, handwriting, listening, reading, math computation, and memory for details. Adults who were not LD in childhood often find themselves stumbling over language processing in ways they never did before. The most noticeable LD characteristic in middle and older age is the slowing pace of mental processing. Intelligence stays the same, but needing more time to respond or to think things through becomes a frustrating pattern for many aging individuals (Atchley, 1990; Salthouse, 1991a; Schieber, 1992).

CHANGES IN HOMEOSTASIS

Executive function relies upon two body control mechanisms: the endocrine system and the central nervous system. Chapter 2 describes how the brain receives new information through the bloodstream and viscera. The bloodstream is primarily a chemical highway that circulates body chemistry messages between individual cells and the brain. This chemical traffic is governed by the endocrine glands (thyroid, pancreas, pituitary, and reproductive organs). In turn, the endocrine glands are controlled by nerve pathways that link all parts of the body with the brain stem, midbrain, and higher brain. When these endocrine and nerve pathway systems perform at normal levels, the body maintains a constant hormonal balance called *homeostasis.* Well-balanced homeostasis is governed by how efficiently the central nervous system delivers data between the brain and the endocrine glands. When all of these components are performing on schedule, we enjoy good thinking and easy learning because of well-balanced homeostasis.

SLOWER EXECUTIVE FUNCTION

In Chapter 2, Figures 2.1 and 2.2 show the dendrite structures that conduct information throughout the brain. Aging produces a variety of changes in dendrites, synapse junctions, and neurotransmitter production (Atchley, 1990; Birren, Sloan, & Cohen, 1992). Sometimes the number of dendrites decreases along major axon pathways. Sometimes extra dendrites appear. These changes in dendrite formation cause changes in the firing speed at which brain regions send and receive information. As individuals grow older, alterations in brain structure slow down the speed of thinking, reacting, making decisions, creating mental images, and remembering. With middle and older age comes slower response time between brain commands, the endocrine system, and muscle reactions. In most adults, aging brings slower executive function. In many adults, aging also brings back LD patterns that were left behind in early adulthood. In many adults, aging brings LD patterns for the first time.

CHANGES IN SLEEP PATTERNS

Chapter 2 describes the team system of the left brain, right brain, and midbrain (see Figure 2.4). A critical factor in how the brain transforms new data into long-term memory is getting enough deep sleep (Damasio, 1994; Schacter, 1996; Shapiro, 1995). During Rapid Eye Movement (REM) cycles of deep sleep, the higher brain sorts through accumulated new information and translates it into memory codes called engrams (see Chapter 2). Over a period of time, failing to get enough deep sleep results in sleep deprivation which interrupts the brain's ability to translate new data into accurate memory codes. As aging advances, most older adults develop problems with sleeping soundly. Prolonged sleep deprivation in older age triggers confusion and inaccurate perceptions that resemble LD in children and adolescents. If poor sleep goes untreated, older adults display symptoms of onset of dimentia. Correcting poor sleep patterns through diet change or medication can restore the higher brain to its normal function of translating new data into long-term memory.

SLOWER COORDINATION

When the brain is young, individuals learn many kinds of physical coordination so well that these motor skills become automatic: walking, turning corners, climbing stairs, handling things, driving vehicles, keyboard writing, workplace routines, athletic skills, using tools and utensils, and so forth. In their mid-50s or early 60s, well-coordinated adults are surprised, sometimes shocked, when they begin to stumble over physical coordination that has been automatic. As aging occurs, adults are forced to think more often about their next moves in order to avoid coordination mistakes. Lack of automatic coordination is a major characteristic of LD for many children and adolescents. Throughout childhood and adolescence, LD persons must think before they act to avoid accidents. Aging brings back this need for cautious action in individuals who had childhood LD, as well as for many adults who have never before had difficulties with coordination.

SLOWER PERCEPTION

In Chapter 2, Figure 2.3 shows the complex process of evaluation that must occur before what the body experiences becomes a mental image. Chapter 2 described how the brain stem examines new sensory data, searching for the presence of danger. Then the midbrain filters out unnecessary information the higher brain does not need to consider. Partly organized bundles of information then are passed to the parietal lobes which classify incoming data and send it on to higher brain regions for full interpretation. Finally comes the moment when the higher brain transforms sensory information into mental images called *perceptions*. Learning disabilities occur when nerve pathways do not work properly in transferring raw data to appropriate regions of the brain. LD occurs when the higher brain cannot create perceptions from raw data it receives. LD forces the brain to detour around roadblocks along information highways throughout the left and right brain hemispheres. Having LD means that one must have extra time, apply extra mental effort, and practice several times before incoming facts are transformed into perceptions. In aging, the speed at which the higher brain perceives slows down for most adults (Atchley, 1990; Birren, Sloan, & Cohen, 1992; Salthouse, 1991a, 1991b; Spirduso & MacRae, 1990).

Making Decisions

One of the first consequences of slower thinking is that the brain needs more time to decide. Throughout life most brain activity is devoted to making decisions. As Chapter 2 explains, every new event is tested automatically for safety. This involves a great deal of mental and emotional energy. As partly organized information reaches the parietal lobes, decisions must be made regarding each bit of data. Where should it be sent? Which brain regions should share this information? Should this new data become coded for long-term memory? Day and night the higher brain makes decisions, and each decision is linked to emotions and feelings. During deep sleep the prefrontal cortex disconnects so that other brain regions can condense volumes of processed data (perceptions) into memory codes. Dreams let us glimpse this coding process, much like scanning rapidly changing cartoons (Damasio, 1994; Schacter, 1996). The basic work of the brain is to decide.

Feeling Safe

Chapter 5 describes the destructive consequences that occur when individuals do not feel safe. Figure 5.1 summarizes the wide range of fear and insecurity that disable many individuals of all ages. Feeling safe is the brain's first priority. Making decisions includes the risk that certain choices might be wrong. To make a decision means that a mistake might be made. Mistakes carry the possibility of danger. It is impossible to make decisions without risking loss of safety. In aging, the process of making decisions slows down. As one enters middle age, it takes longer to decide. It is not safe to rush the decision-making process. What if a vital safety factor is overlooked? What if an important detail is left out by hurrying? This emotional agenda becomes increasingly critical for individuals who were LD in early years. Having learning disability means that making decisions is done cautiously, or else the individual lives in a state of dread or actual fear. To be sure becomes the central issue in making decisions as one ages. Adults who had quick decision-making habits during early adulthood find themselves acting or reacting more cautiously as they near age 60 and older. Aging brains need more time to transform raw data into perceptions. This process cannot be rushed without triggering strong apprehension or even fear of making decisions. As adults age, they become overly cautious, often refusing to decide rather than take risks that would not have been a problem in youth.

Higher Threshold of Response to Stimulus

For new data to reach the higher brain, a certain level of stimulus must be experienced. This can be compared with the level of pressure a keyboard must receive before individual keys trigger response in the computer or on the typewriter. For example, I have three keyboard systems on which I write. Each keyboard requires a different degree of pressure for my finger taps to send information into the computer system. One keyboard responds instantly to light touch. Another requires heavy finger pressure before the keys respond. The third keyboard responds to moderate finger pressure, except for the space bar, which must be tapped with extra force. In a similar way, the many sensory organs that feed information to the brain have varying levels of sensitivity. To listen, some individuals require a lot of oral stimulus, or else they do not respond. To respond to instructions, some persons must have extra stimulus through eye contact and hearing new information again. Some individuals are acutely sensitive to being touched, while others do not feel a touch unless it is applied with some force. Most individuals enjoy the thunderous music of a pipe organ, while others cover their ears against "all that noise." These differences in how we respond to stimulus are called the *threshold of sensory response.* Aging brings about changes in the threshold of sensory response. As most adults enter middle age and older years, they must have stronger stimulus to respond. The threshold of sensory response increases as the brain ages.

LD and Stimulus Threshold

A major characteristic of LD is the need for extra stimulus before the brain makes sense of new information. This is why most LD learners do better when several sensory pathways (modalities) are involved. Persons who are LD usually need to hear it, say it, and feel or touch it, all at the same time, before their brains develop perceptions of phonics, spelling patterns, word pronunciations, and math computation. As aging occurs, most older adults find themselves needing more stimulus to form complete mental images and memory for new information.

DIFFERENCES BETWEEN LD AND DEMENTIA

As adults enter old age, it is important for caregivers and companions to recognize the differences between LD and other types of changes in how the brain functions. Deterioration in brain structures, called organic mental disorders, are not the same as LD. Breakdown in the quality of mental activity is generally called *dementia.* The Decade of the Brain has revealed that 55% of the aging population will slip into the shadows of Alzheimer's disease in older age (Atchley, 1990). From 4 to 8% of the aging population will require care because of dementia (Raskind & Peskind, 1992). Dementia is caused by progressive and irreversible breakdown in neurons, axon pathways, synapse junctions, and dendrite structures. As this invisible deterioration of brain regions occurs, dementia is manifested by the following symptoms:

1. Mental confusion
2. Incoherent speech
3. Loss of short-term and long-term memory
4. Loss of orientation in one's environment
5. Agitated behavior
6. Excessive worrying and fretting
7. Depression
8. Loss of motor coordination
9. Increasing hallucinations
10. Cycles of fearful delusions and delirium
11. Loss of intelligence

LD in older adults may at first appear to be onset of dementia. However, there are major differences between the behaviors of LD and those of dementia.

1. Forgetfulness in daily routines
2. Increasing difficulty in language processing
3. Requiring more stimulus to understand oral information
4. Losing one's thoughts and words while speaking
5. Increasing errors in spelling
6. Increasing difficult with reading accuracy and comprehension
7. Increasing problems with handwriting
8. Needing more time to decide
9. Nervousness or fearfulness when pressed to hurry
10. Increasing resistance to changes in routines
11. Growing concern for feeling safe
12. Needing more time to finish tasks
13. Needing help to stay on schedules and keep appointments
14. Increasing need to talk to oneself while doing tasks
15. Retention of intelligence

MANAGING LD IN AGING ADULTS

Of whatever age, most adults who have LD learn to manage life issues on their own. Only severe learning difficulties, such as severe dyslexia or ADHD, force LD adults to have help in order to live independently. LD throughout adulthood is largely a matter of self-management. Certain strategies are essential in the lifestyle of LD adults.

Patient Understanding

Far more than financial support as one ages is the need for patient understanding. This chapter has described critical ways in which lifestyle changes as the brain grows older. Needing more time, feeling anxious in making decisions, being fearful or unsure of one's own judgments, keeping track of everything, remembering appointments—all of these issues contain the seeds of shame. Chapter 5 reviewed James Gilligan's concept that shame underlies most of the violence he sees in prison populations. Gilligan's model of behavior modification recognizes the powerful impact of shame. This is equally important for aging adults, especially when LD exists. Saving face, protecting one's dignity, and avoiding shame and humiliation are perhaps the deepest needs for all of us as we enter the years of growing old.

Reminder Systems

Adults with LD must keep track of obligations, appointments, and other scheduled events. This is most easily done by carrying a pocket calendar on which all events are noted. As the brain ages, outside reminding from a spouse, companion, friend, or colleague becomes a necessary part of one's lifestyle. Every day or so, the other person spends a few minutes helping the LD adult review the calendar, making sure that immediate events are not overlooked or forgotten. Whoever does this reminding also leaves phone messages and e-mail reminders, if the LD person has access to telecommunications. This reminding always is friendly, never critical. The purpose is to help aging LD individuals retain dignity and avoid humiliation that comes through habitual forgetting.

Enough Time

A critical need of LD adults is to have enough time to think things through, develop mental concepts and perceptions, retrieve information from memory, and make safe decisions. Chapter 5 describes the impact that fear and uncertainty have on higher brain functions. As the brain ages, it becomes increasingly important that enough time be allowed without feeling pressed to hurry. As much as possible, adults with LD must develop time management plans that guarantee having enough time. As aging progresses, the LD adult's schedule must be simplified so that the most important tasks are completed successfully. This often involves learning to say "no" to events that would be nice, but are not necessary. To avoid depression and anxiety, the aging brain must have enough time to feel safe.

Help Correcting Mistakes

It is important for LD individuals to have the opportunity to correct their own mistakes. As the brain ages, the ability to spot one's own errors declines. As mistakes increase, LD adults need help to identify and correct their errors. Memory for correct spelling begins to decline, which calls for another pair of eyes to scan written work for mistakes. Recall of specific details becomes less reliable, which requires help in remembering exactly. Paying bills on time, keeping track of business papers, balancing the checkbook, making bank deposits, or keeping a grocery list become major sources of anxiety and embarrassment for aging adults who try to do it all alone. As errors occur in these life tasks, someone must step in to offer quiet, friendly suggestions on how to correct mistakes.

CHAPTER 7

What the Future Holds

KNOWLEDGE OF BRAIN FUNCTIONS

In November 1998, John Gabrieli at Stanford University's Department of Psychology announced the development of a brain scan technique that can identify which individuals have Attention Deficit Disorder (ADD) (Recer, 1998). A new generation of brain imaging technology called functional Magnetic Resonant Imaging (fMRI) can watch portions of the limbic system at work during attention-based tasks. Gabrieli discovered what he calls the "ADD signature" in the basal ganglia (see Figure 2.4). This new generation of brain imaging science (fMRI) permitted Sally Shaywitz to describe how the left brain reads (see Figure 1.1) (Shaywitz, 1996). Figure 1.3 presents Paula Tallal's fMRI mapping of how the midbrain (medial geniculate nucleus) sorts and organizes speech sounds. Chapter 2 reviews the research by Damasio and Schachter into how the brain deals with emotions and feelings first before attending to facts. These and other neurological discoveries suggest that in the next century a great deal more will be discovered about neurological functions through improved brain imaging techniques. These intriguing new insights into how the brain learns and remembers bring good news for those who struggle with learning disabilities. Soon it will become feasible to design teaching techniques based upon how each person's brain processes language, or fails to do so. During most of my career, finding the best teaching and learning techniques has been by trial and error. In the next century, teaching and learning will be based upon how individual brains learn, or fail to learn.

ALTERING PROGRAMS IN THE BRAIN

Stretched Speech for Tone Deaf Listeners

Until the Decade of the Brain, most of us assumed that the adult brain cannot be changed. We believed that whatever neurological patterns a person brings into adulthood will remain that way through old age. Efforts to teach language skills to dyslexic individuals were based upon the premise that LD must be compensated for or accommodated because missing links between brain regions are forever beyond change or repair. As the Decade of the Brain got underway, Michael Merzenich at the University of California in San Francisco reported an astonishing discovery about the plasticity of the brain in mature individuals (Travis, 1996). Merzenich found a type of "learning disability" in some adult monkeys in his research lab. These mature animals had the same kind of auditory deficit that Tallal discovered in "tone deaf" dyslexic individuals (see Figure 1.3). These monkeys could not respond to fast sounds because of deficits in how the auditory cortex was wired. On a hunch, Merzenich developed a brain stimulus technique that stretched out the typical 40 millisecond duration of the missing sound responses. Later the brains of these experimental monkeys were analyzed. Merzenich discovered that stimulating the auditory cortex through stretched sound practice had reorganized the neural circuits within the medial geniculate nucleus where sounds are processed. Stimulating that region of the brain through stretched sound activity had changed brain structure so that the monkeys could perceive the missing fast sound chunks.

This unexpected experience in changing mature brain structure through stimulation led Merzenich to collaborate with Paula Tallal, Robert Fitch, and Steven Miller at Rutgers University (Tallal et al, 1993). This team developed a brain-stimulus technique that produced "stretched speech." By extending the duration of difficult speech sounds (phonemes) by 50% at the same time the volume was increased, Tallal and Miller developed oral stories with exaggerated speech that sounds peculiar to most listeners. However, for "tone deaf" dyslexic persons, those stretched speech presentations sounded normal for the first time. With this brain

stimulus technique, dyslexic listeners could hear differences between "pack" and "packed," "idea" and "ideal," "thermos" and
"furnace," and so forth. At the end of the experimental time, the
dyslexic listeners showed a 2-year increase in oral language skills.
Tone deaf listeners who had been taught by conventional meth-
ods had gained 6 months. This early research has not answered the
question: Can human brain structure be changed through stimulus? However, this brain research shows that with appropriate re-
mediation that is tailored to specific brain deficits, dyslexic learners can be taught language skills they cannot learn any other way.

Correcting Scotopic Sensitivity Syndrome

As research by Livingstone, Lehmkuhle, and Eden became
widely known (see Figure 1.11), brain scientists asked if adding
color through the Irlen Procedure had any effect upon brain function. In 1993, Livingstone conducted some studies of Scotopic
adults. Using fMRI brain imaging, she recorded how the magnocellular pathway and geniculate nucleus worked while the person
experienced the print distortions shown in Figure 1.10. Then Livingstone repeated the brain scan while the Scotopic individual
wore colored lenses (Irlen filters). To her surprise, Livingstone
saw differences on the fMRI that indicated change in brain function when Scotopic Sensitivity syndrome was treated through
color application (Livingstone, personal correspondence, March
14, 1993).

Information Processing

Chapter 5 describes shadow syndromes that often hide beneath the surface of learning difficulties. Brain science has discovered that the brain is designed to cope with stress and emotional trauma (Damasio, 1994; Ratey & Johnson, 1997; Schacter,
1996; Shapiro, 1995). Figure 2.3 in Chapter 2 shows the sequence
of how new data is processed by the brain. Before any new facts
are considered, the brain stem asks: "Is this safe?" New events
that present risk of emotional harm are dealt with first. In nor-

mally developed brains, stressful or threatening events finally are resolved through a neurological sequence called *information processing*. Over time if the person has enough rest and does not experience too much new stress, the brain replaces strong first emotions with logical reasoning. Engrams that store high-risk memories are modified so that future memory does not stir up anxiety or fear.

This problem-solving ability of the brain often is thwarted when stressful new events are overpowering. For example, children with unrecognized LD frequently are so frightened by classroom expectations they develop phobic response to school learning. Thousands of Vietnam war veterans came home with Post Traumatic Stress Disorder that has continued at nightmare levels in their private lives. Individuals who are overly sensitive to stress become victims of mental illness that is linked to unresolved anxiety and fear. Childhood victims of sexual or physical abuse may carry nightmare memories all their lives. Manic/depressive adults carry unresolved lifelong terrors in the shadows of their lives. Traditional psychotherapy often cannot free these suffering individuals from their hidden fears.

Eye Movement Desensitization and Reprocessing

In 1979 Francine Shapiro made an accidental discovery that became the well-researched technique called *EMDR* (Eye Movement Desensitization and Reprocessing). During a time of personal stress over unresolved emotional shadows, Shapiro discovered that rapidly moving her eyes back and forth while focusing upward as she thought about distressing personal issues decreased the level of her anxiety (Shapiro, 1995). In fact, when she repeated rapid eye movements while pondering stressful memories, Shapiro became free from the bondage of chronic anxiety. This technique allowed her to think through old issues and resolve painful events that she had not been able to deal with previously. EMDR involves far more than shifting the eyes rapidly. Before starting rapid eye movement therapy, persons think through shadow syndromes that cause the most emotional pain. With practice, they learn how to concentrate on specific unresolved problems while doing rapid eye movement exercises. As the eyes sprint back and forth, the brain reviews the facts wrapped inside old frightful emotions. This process simultaneously stimulates several regions of the left brain, right brain, and midbrain. This multimodality activity allows the prefrontal cortex to replace strong, destructive emotions from the limbic system with higher emotions that bring logical resolution to old dyslogical issues. As we enter the new century, EMDR shows great promise for setting LD adults free from lifelong fear of learning. Brain stimulus through Shapiro's EMDR technique reprograms enough engrams to permit LD individuals to approach learning for the first time without being afraid.

DIAGNOSIS OF LD IN ADULTS

The diagnosis of learning disabilities in adults is shrouded in strong controversy. Two schools of thought are in conflict over how LD should be determined. On one hand, many professionals insist that a rigorous standard be maintained in determining the presence of LD. This point of view requires that struggling learners undergo standardized psycho-educational evaluation that produces clusters of standard scores from tests of intelligence and achievement (Ackerman et al., 1997; Barkley et al., 1991; Ingersoll & Goldstein, 1993; Wechsler, 1994; Woodcock, 1991). For LD to be recognized, the student must have an arbitrary discrepancy between measured IQ and standard scores in reading skills, written languages skills, spelling, and math. This school of thought pays no attention to symptoms of dyslexia, dysgraphia, dyscalculia, ADHD, or ADD until after score discrepancy shows the statistical probability that an individual is LD. Complicating the LD issue further is the fact that each school district in the United States, as well as each governing agency, may set different score discrepancy standards. Thus, an adult who is legally LD in Texas might not be LD in Utah or New York because of differences in how much discrepancy each person must show in standard score comparisons.

On the other hand, an opposite school of thought insists that we cannot determine the presence of LD by test scores alone

(Denckla, 1993; Hammill & Bryant, 1998; Jordan, 1996a, 1998; Kauffman & Hallahan, 1996; Naglieri & Reardon, 1993). This point of view begins by asking: How does the learner struggle with classroom tasks? Diagnosis of LD begins by building a portfolio of LD symptoms, as shown in Chapter 1. Observations are accumulated from instructors, tutors, and others who have worked one-on-one in skill development with the struggling learner. Finally, standard tests of intelligence and achievement might be given to gather statistical verification of LD.

Informal Assessment of LD in Adults

As we discover more about brain functions and learning, informal assessment that shows the symptoms of LD will become increasingly important. For example, the *Jordan Dyslexia Assessment/Reading Program* is a widely used informal assessment throughout adult education (Jordan, 1999). This program offers a variety of screening instruments that show symptoms of visual dyslexia, auditory dyslexia, dysgraphia, ADHD, ADD, and NVLD (Nonverbal LD) in adults. The Jordan Program includes step-by-step instruction in teaching basic reading skills to adults who are dyslexic. Figure 1.2 in Chapter 1 shows how another widely used informal LD assessment inventory brings dyslexia to the surface: the *Slingerland Screening Tests for Identifying Children with Specific Language Disabilities*. The Jordan and Slingerland assessment inventories are examples of nonthreatening LD evaluation techniques that will gain momentum as adult education moves into the new century.

Standardized Assessment of LD in Adults

As we enter the next century, only one standardized test exists specifically designed to identify LD in adults. All other current tests for learning disabilities in adults are derived from tests for children. Starting in 1975, Laura Weisel has constructed an LD diagnostic test specifically designed for adults (Weisel, 1992). Weisel's *POWERPath to Adult Basic Learning* is a fully standardized instrument that discovers how the brain processes a variety of information. This diagnostic procedure evaluates eyesight, hearing, auditory perception, visual perception, and a range of motor skills that are linked to literacy. POWERPath identifies forms of dyslexia, attention deficit disorders, and Scotopic Sensitivity syndrome. The most important feature of POWERPath is the way in which LD adults feel safe doing these procedures. Virtually no school phobias are triggered as apprehensive LD adults do the POWERPath evaluation.

PLANTING HOPE IN THE PLACE OF DESPAIR

As I say in the preface, this book is about replacing crushed spirits with cheerful hearts. As we enter the new century, adults who struggle with LD have a great deal of hope that a cheerful heart will indeed replace despair in learning. Knowing what the problem is starts the struggling learner up the path toward emotional freedom. Knowing how each brain functions, or fails to function, will guide future instructors in matching individuals with appropriate strategies and techniques. Learning that "I'm not dumb!" is the most important factor in guiding LD persons toward freedom from old fears. In the decades to come, many crushed spirits will rise with the joy of a cheerful heart as the information in this book becomes widely acknowledged.

APPENDIX A

Guidebooks for Managing LD in Adults

Alexander-Roberts, Colleen. *ADHD & Teens: A Parent's Guide to Making It through the Rough Years.* (Dallas, TX: Taylor Publishing Company, 1995).

Fowler, Mary C. *"Honey Are You Listening?": How Attention Deficit Disorder Could Be Affecting Your Marriage.* (Nashville, TN: Thomas Nelson, Inc., 1995).

Hallowell, Edward M., & Ratey, John J. *Driven to Distraction: Recognizing and Coping with Attention Deficit Disorder from Childhood through Adulthood.* (New York: Pantheon Books, 1994).

Hallowell, Edward M., & Ratey, John J. *Answers to Distraction.* (New York: Pantheon Books, 1994).

Jordan, Dale R. *Overcoming Dyslexia in Children, Adolescents, and Adults.* (Austin, TX: PRO-ED, 1996).

Jordan, Dale R. *Attention Deficit Disorder: ADHD & ADD Syndromes in Children, Adolescents, and Adults.* (Austin, TX: PRO-ED, 1998).

Jordan, Dale R. *Teaching Adults with Learning Disabilities.* (Malabar, FL: Krieger Publishing Company, 1996).

Quinn, Patricia O. *ADD and the College Student: A Guide for High School and College Students with Attention Deficit Disorder.* (Grass Valley, CA: Underwood Books, 1995).

Ratey, John J., & Johnson, Catherine. *Shadow Syndromes.* (New York: Pantheon Books, 1997).

Weiss, Lynn. *A.D.D. On the Job: Making Your A.D.D. Work for You.* (Dallas, TX: Taylor Publishing Company, 1995.

Weiss, Lynn. *Attention Deficit Disorder in Adults: Practical Help for Sufferers and Their Spouses.* (Dallas, TX: Taylor Publishing Company, 1992).

Weiss, Lynn. *The Attention Deficit Disorder in Adults Workbook.* (Dallas, TX: Taylor Publishing Company, 1994).

APPENDIX B

Jordan Index for Asperger's Syndrome

The *Jordan Index for Asperger's Syndrome* is designed to estimate individual levels of severity for this form of Nonverbal LD. It is unlikely that an adult with Asperger's symptoms could do this index as a self-evaluation activity. A major deficit of Asperger's is the inability to see oneself objectively. This index is intended to be the basis for organizing what is observed by others. The Jordan Index presents 22 behaviors that are characteristic of Asperger's syndrome. Following each behavior are four columns: *Never, Sometimes, Usually,* and *Always.* Each column is given a score. The rater places a check in the column that best reflects the person's behavior in that area. To estimate the individual's level of severity, a subscore is obtained for each column. This is done by totalling all the checks within the column. For example, each check in the *Sometimes* column is worth 1. Each check in the *Usually* column is worth 2. Each check in the *Always* column is worth 3. After the subscores are figured, they are added together to find the TOTAL SCORE. Then the TOTAL SCORE is transferred to the appropriate place in the *Asperger's Syndrome Profile.* The Rating Scale gives a quick reference to where the individual ranks on the severity scale. The descriptive paragraphs summarize the lifestyle of this person. The Jordan Index indicates how disruptive this individual is likely to be in the workplace, the classroom, or in personal relationships.

JORDAN INDEX FOR ASPERGER'S SYNDROME

	Never 0	Sometimes 1	Usually 2	Always 3
1. *Awkward gross motor development.*	____	____	____	____

	Never 0	Sometimes 1	Usually 2	Always 3
Awkward when standing around, walking, running, hopping, skipping, playing ball				
2. *Pedantic speech.* Voice doesn't relax into conversational tone. Speech is slow and deliberate like giving a boring lecture	___	___	___	___
3. *Voice has flat tone.* Voice inflection doesn't rise and fall in natural vocal rhythms	___	___	___	___
4. *Awkward at small talk.* Can't think of anything to say at parties or when introduced to new people. Struggles to turn knowledge into chit-chat	___	___	___	___
5. *Too slow at thinking of something to say.* Later thinks of something, but too late to fit into conversation	___	___	___	___
6. *Restricted sense of humor.* Doesn't get the point of jokes. Misses the point of friendly teasing. Bristles at friendly teasing. Can't repeat or tell jokes effectively	___	___	___	___
7. *Stiff awkward body posture.* Doesn't relax when standing around or sitting. Seems to be posing instead of being at ease	___	___	___	___
8. *Excellent recall of trivial details.* Is a specialist in a few narrow issues. Drones on and on about trivial details that don't interest others	___	___	___	___
9. *Very narrow range of interests.* Has one or two topics he/she works to death. Doesn't expand to new or more interesting topics	___	___	___	___

	Never 0	Sometimes 1	Usually 2	Always 3
10. *Extreme splitter.* Overanalyzes. Can't let loose ends go. Constantly splits, then splits the splits. Corrects others when they don't say or do exactly so	___	___	___	___
11. *Triggers dread in others.* Others try to avoid conversations with this person. Others make excuses not to be involved with this person	___	___	___	___
12. *Boring personality.* Nothing is socially interesting about this person. Others soon glance at the time and try to move away	___	___	___	___
13. *Inappropriate social habits.* Personal habits are embarrassing or obnoxious. Doesn't learn better manners. Doesn't change inappropriate behavior	___	___	___	___
14. *Behavior is ritualized, often eccentric.* This person lives by rigid rituals. Others call him/her "weird." Behavior is obsessive. Can't stop doing same things over and over	___	___	___	___
15. *Doesn't read social signals.* Doesn't recognize signals to "back off," "give me a break," "not now." Barges in when others want to be left alone	___	___	___	___
16. *A chronic controller.* Uses wide range of control strategies. Is a poor member of committees or work teams. Has poor sense of deferring to needs or wishes of others. Tries to isolate certain individuals to keep them away from influence of others	___	___	___	___

	Never 0	Sometimes 1	Usually 2	Always 3
17. *Habitually rationalizes.* Explains away own mistakes and poor judgment. Blames others. Fixes responsibility on others when things go wrong	____	____	____	____
18. *Does best work when alone in highly structured tasks that don't change.*	____	____	____	____
19. *Is creative within narrow range of interests.* Has reputation of being an "eccentric genius" if left alone in own territory or work space	____	____	____	____
20. *Doesn't know when to stop.* Talks or writes on and on and on. Doesn't recognize normal stopping places or when enough has been said	____	____	____	____
21. *Has unrealistic or grandiose hopes for success or fame.* Talks about writing the great novel, producing sensational screen plays, making a million dollars, or otherwise becoming famous	____	____	____	____
22. *Is stubborn in situations that require flexibility.* Clings stubbornly to ritualized habits. Refuses to change. Argues against change	____	____	____	____

Add up the value of all the checks in each column to find the subscore for each column.

Subscores _____ _____ _____

Add the subscores to find the TOTAL SCORE.

TOTAL SCORE _____

Transfer TOTAL SCORE to the Rating Scale and appropriate paragraph sections in the ASPERGER'S SYNDROME PROFILE.

ASPERGER'S SYNDROME PROFILE

Rating Scale

0 to 11 none	12 to 25 mild	26 to 40 moderate severe	41 to 55 moderately	Above 55 severe

_____	0 to 11	Not enough habits to be called Asperger's syndrome
_____	12 to 25	Mild Asperger's syndrome

Is moderately boring in conversation. Social behavior is noticeably awkward as if he/she has not been taught good manners. Is noticeably self-focused. Talks about self and personal interests more than he/she pays attention to others. Has narrow range of interests, but can briefly tune into interests of others when reminded. Can work with others if the team has a firm, patient leader. Prefers to work alone in own space. Has sets of ritualized habits that are repeated without adding new habits. Has noticeably good memory for details in areas of personal interest. Soon begins to irritate workmates, classmates, and new acquaintances. Flat droning voice soon irritates others.

Can be guided toward more appropriate behavior if guidance is patient and nonjudgmental. Can learn to tone down Asperger's patterns if undesirable behaviors are listed in writing. Can memorize more appropriate behavior patterns like learning a role in a play.

_____	26 to 40	Moderate Asperger's syndrome

Behavior is considered strange or "weird," but can be tolerated by most colleagues or associates. Is boring in all situations. Is considered very competent in one or two areas of work. Launches into boring, pedantic monologues whenever he/she is alone with anyone. Manners are noticeably irregular and often crude. Lifestyle is ritualized and inflexible with habits repeated over and over without change. Body posture and motions are awkward and stiff. Obviously lacks a sense of humor. Effort to tell jokes is often embarrassing to others. Effort to make small talk is often painful for others to watch.

Resists attempts by others to modify behaviors or expand interests. Resists any change that would involve modifying rituals and habits. Argues against change. Tends to blame others for own mistakes. Puts more energy and time into rationalizing than into developing new skills or procedures. Becomes offended by advice from supervisors or colleagues about changing habits or modifying behavior.

| | 41 to 55 | Moderately Severe Asperger's syndrome |

Distinctly "weird" in general behavior. Cannot carry on conversations without launching into self-centered monologues about one or two narrow topics. Flat, droning voice quickly irritates others. Others dread, try to avoid this person. Is a chronic controller and manipulator. Lifestyle is highly ritualized with many eccentric behaviors. Has rigidly inflexible habits and attitudes. Continually argues when asked to accept different or new ideas. Spouts streams of trivial information that bores and exasperates others. Is a poor member of teams or committees because of rigid attitudes and inflexibility. Habitually blames others for own mistakes. Loses much valuable time splitting hairs over unimportant issues.

Openly resists or sabotages efforts to upgrade, change, or modify job procedures. Cannot be relied upon to follow through on new procedures. Manners are generally obnoxious and unpleasant. Flat, monotone voice is a major source of irritation. Triggers much conflict and contention in work groups or study groups.

Rarely responds to counseling or other efforts to bring about change. Is extremely sensitive, often paranoid, toward constructive criticism. Is a very poor risk for behavior modification.

—— | Above 55 | Severe Asperger's syndrome

Asperger's patterns are overwhelming. Impossible for this person to fit into social groups. Is seldom possible for this person to succeed in work groups. Behavior is so irregular, rigid, obnoxious, "weird," that others shun and avoid. Personal habits are offensive. Has virtually no tact or social amenities. Is almost totally self-centered and blind to needs or interests of others. Is hostile to change. Is surly and rude when others suggest that he/she should change. Habitually blames others for own mistakes. Devotes much time to rationalizing and blaming.

Struggles to find employment. Cannot do job interviews successfully. May be well educated, but is too irregular and offensive to be employed. May do satisfactory work in a highly structured job in private space away from others.

Is actively resistant to/suspicious of counseling or guidance. There is virtually no hope that counseling might modify or improve personality patterns or behaviors.

APPENDIX C

Jordan Executive Function Inventory

The *Jordan Executive Function Inventory* is designed to show the levels of efficiency in how a person organizes, pays attention, and maintains self-control. Adults who read well can do this inventory as a self-evaluation activity. Others can participate in an interview activity by listening to each item, then selecting the appropriate column response. The *Jordan Executive Function Inventory* presents 30 behaviors in three categories: *Organization, Attention,* and *Inhibition.* Following each item are four columns: *Never, Sometimes, Usually,* and *Always.* Each column is given a score. The rater places a check in the column that best reflects the person's behavior in that area. To estimate the individual's level of efficiency, a subscore is obtained for each column. This is done by totalling the checks within the column. For example, each check in the *Sometimes* column is worth 1. Each check in the *Usually* column is worth 2. Each check in the *Always* column is worth 3. After the subscores are figured, they are added together to find the TOTAL SCORE for that page. Then the three TOTAL SCORES are added together to find the FINAL TOTAL SCORE. This FINAL TOTAL SCORE is entered in the appropriate place on the *Jordan Executive Function Profile.* The Rating Scale gives a quick reference to the person's level of efficiency in executive function. The paragraphs summarize the lifestyle and work style, as well as predicting how successful the individual is likely to be in the workplace or classroom.

JORDAN EXECUTIVE FUNCTION INVENTORY

Organization	Never 0	Sometimes 1	Usually 2	Always 3
1. Keeps personal space organized and tidy without reminding	_____	_____	_____	_____

	Never 0	Sometimes 1	Usually 2	Always 3
2. Keeps workplace organized and tidy without reminding	___	___	___	___
3. Keeps vehicle clean and tidy without reminding	___	___	___	___
4. Keeps track of things without reminding	___	___	___	___
5. Is on time for scheduled appointments without reminding	___	___	___	___
6. Keeps track of future commitments without reminding	___	___	___	___
7. Remembers birthdays, holidays, anniversaries without reminding	___	___	___	___
8. Manages own money without reminding	___	___	___	___
9. Plans ahead for necessary supplies at home, work, and school without reminding	___	___	___	___
10. Understands how things should be organized at work, home, and school without reminding	___	___	___	___
SUBSCORES		___	___	___
TOTAL SCORE	___			

Attention	Never 0	Sometimes 1	Usually 2	Always 3
1. Keeps on listening without becoming distracted or sidetracked	___	___	___	___
2. Follows what is going on without becoming distracted or sidetracked	___	___	___	___
3. Listens without interrupting until the full message has been spoken	___	___	___	___

	Never 0	Sometimes 1	Usually 2	Always 3
4. Stays on task until it is finished without becoming distracted or sidetracked	____	____	____	____
5. Finishes what is started without being reminded to keep on working	____	____	____	____
6. Ignores nearby disruptions without leaving task to investigate or join in	____	____	____	____
7. Notices and responds to needs of others without neglecting own tasks and responsibilities	____	____	____	____
8. Stays involved with events without leaving task to investigate or join in	____	____	____	____
9. Has consistent memory of events and information without gaps in what has happened or been taught	____	____	____	____
10. Is on task with lifestyle, on target in decision making, good at listening and paying attention, good at finishing what is started	____	____	____	____

SUBSCORES _____ _____ _____

TOTAL SCORE _____

Inhibition (Self-Control)

	Never 0	Sometimes 1	Usually 2	Always 3
1. Willingly puts off wishes and desires for a better time	____	____	____	____
2. Willingly cooperates when plans must be changed	____	____	____	____
3. Willingly yields to needs and wishes of others	____	____	____	____
4. Says "no" or "wait" to impulses	____	____	____	____

	Never 0	Sometimes 1	Usually 2	Always 3
5. Plans ahead, then willingly follows through on plans without impatience	____	____	____	____
6. Exercises logic and common sense reasoning in making decisions	____	____	____	____
7. Considers consequences before acting	____	____	____	____
8. Learns from mistakes. Changes behavior from lessons learned	____	____	____	____
9. Seeks and accepts good advice when not sure of how to decide	____	____	____	____
10. Lifestyle is governed by logic, common sense, putting off pleasure until the best time, exercising control over impulses, thinking of consequences before acting	____	____	____	____

SUBSCORES ____ ____ ____

TOTAL SCORE ____

FINAL TOTAL SCORE ____

JORDAN EXECUTIVE FUNCTION PROFILE

Rating Scale

0 through 10	11 through 19	20 through 59	60 through 78	Above 78
Severe Deficits in Executive	Moderately Severe Deficits in Executive Function	Moderate Deficits in Executive Function	Mild Deficits in Executive Function	No Significant Deficits in Executive Function

____ SEVERE DEFICITS in Executive Function

Cannot fit into workplace or classroom. Behavior is too disruptive, too abrasive, too oppositional to follow rules of conduct. Cannot maintain personal relationships. Too self-focused to see needs or wishes of others. Too rigid and inflexible to accept guidance to modify disruptive behavior. Cannot see why others find fault or criticize. Hair-trigger temper explodes under criticism or pressure to change. Needs supervision to get by in life, but is too touchy to accept guidance. Does not think logically or use common sense. Lives by intense emotions that serve self first. Cannot wait or postpone personal desires. Lives by impulse. Is severely forgetful. Lifestyle has no organization, self-discipline, or attention to issues apart from self. Has no long-term sense of responsibility apart from satisfying self.

_____ MODERATELY SEVERE DEFICITS in Executive Function

Can develop competency in job skills and classroom learning if he/she finds a comfortable place that allows freedom to be different. Has history of short job tenure. Has started and dropped out of several educational programs. Has very poor social skills, but often has a few friends who also have deficits in Executive Function. Occasionally accepts guidance and constructive criticism from someone he/she trusts. Must have help managing money. Must have "supervisor" who reminds and helps this person stay on track and meet commitments. Is overly forgetful. Continually loses or misplaces things. Must have one or two others who are willing to absorb tantrums, frustrations, and restlessness. Must have "new mercies" over and over from others who can forgive lifestyle differences.

_____ MODERATE DEFICITS in Executive Function

May have good job skills. May have college degree. Lives with continual frustration and frequent conflict in workplace, classroom, and home. May have a few lasting friendships with others who are patient and forgiving. Needs frequent help gathering up loose ends of unfinished tasks, reorganizing personal space, and maintaining order in personal space. Depends upon pocket calendars and other visual reminders to stay on schedule. Is forgetful and misplaces things. Often regarded as "careless airhead" because of so many mistakes.

———————— MILD DEFICITS in Executive Function

Is successful in workplace, school, and home, but has enough problems remembering, keeping track of things, and staying organized to be frustrated much of the time. Lifestyle is loose and poorly organized. With effort, he/she compensates for memory irregularities well enough to maintain relationships and good work history. Struggles to stay on schedule, remember appointments and commitments, finish what is started, and resist distractions.

———————— NO SIGNIFICANT DEFICITS in Executive Function

REFERENCES

Ackerman, P. T., Dykman, R. A., & Peters, J. E. (1997). Teenage status of hyperactive and nonhyperactive learning disabled boys. *American Journal of Orthopsychiatry, 47,* 577–596.

Alexander-Roberts, C. (1995). *ADHD and teens: A parent's guide to making it through the tough years.* Dallas, TX: Taylor.

American Psychiatric Association. (1980). *Diagnostic and statistical manual of mental disorders* (3rd ed.), Washington, DC: Author.

American Psychiatric Association. (1994). *Diagnostic and statistical manual of mental disorders* (4th ed.), Washington, DC: Author.

Atchley, R. C., (Ed.). (1994). *Social forces and aging* (7th ed.). Belmont, CA: Wadsworth.

Bain, L. J. (1991). *A parent's guide to attention deficit disorders.* New York: Dell.

Barkley, R. A. (1990). *Attention-deficit hyperactivity disorder: A handbook for diagnosis and treatment.* New York: Guilford.

Barkley, R. A. (1995). *Taking charge of ADHD: The complete, authoritative guide for parents.* New York: Guilford.

Barkley, R. A., Spitzer, R., & Costello, A. (1991). *Development of the DSM-III-R criteria for the disruptive behavior disorders.* Unpublished manuscript, University of Massachusetts Medical Center, Worcester.

Berlin, R. (1884). Uber Dyslexie [About Dyslexia]. *Archiv Für Psychiatrie, 15,* 276–278.

Berlin, R. (1887). *Einebosondere Art der Wortblindheit: Dyslexia* [A special type of wordblindness: Dyslexia]. Wiesbaden: J. F. Bergmann.

Birren, J. E., Sloane, B., & Cohen, G. D. (Eds.). (1992). *Handbook of mental health and aging* (2nd ed.). New York: Academic Press.

Charness, N., & Bosman, E. A. (1992). Human factors and aging. In F. I. M. Craik & T. A. Salthouse (Eds.), *The handbook of aging and cognition* (pp. 495–552). Hillsdale, NJ: Lawrence Erlbaum Associates.

Connors, C. K. (1990). *Feeding the brain: How foods affect children.* New York: Plenum Press.

Copeland, E. D. (1991). *Medicines for attention disorders (ADHD/ADD) and related medical problems.* Atlanta, GA: 3 C's of Childhood, Inc.

Damasio, A. R. (1994). *Descartes' error: emotion, reason, and the human brain.* New York: Avon Books.

Damasio, A. R. (1995, November 12). Sex hormones key in brain development. *Tulsa World,* p. A7.

Denckla, M. B. (1978). Minimal brain dysfunction. In J. S. Chall & A. F. Mirsky (Eds.), *Education and the brain* (pp. 223–268). Chicago: University of Chicago Press.

Denckla, M. B. (1983). The neuropsychology of social-emotional learning disabilities. *Archives of Neurology, 40:461–462.*

Denckla, M. B. (1991a). Academic and extracurricular aspects of nonverbal learning disabilities. *Psychiatric Annals, 21:717–724.*

Denckla, M. B. (1991b, March). *The neurology of social competence.* Paper presented at the Learning Disabilities Association national conference, Chicago.

Denckla, M. B. (1993). The child with developmental disabilities grown up: Adult residua of childhood disorders. *Behavioral Neurology, 11*(1), 105–125.

Duane, D. (1985, November). *Psychiatric implications of neurological difficulties.* Symposium conducted at the Menninger Foundation, Topeka, KS.

Duane, D. (1987, November). *The anatomy of dyslexia and neurobiology of human aptitude.* Symposium conducted by the Orton Dyslexia Society, San Francisco.

Eden, G. F. (1996, November). *Visualizing vision in dyslexic brains.* Symposium conducted by Society for Neuroscience, San Diego.

Fisher, B. J. (1992). Successful aging and life satisfaction: A pilot study for conceptual clarification. *Journal of Aging Studies, 6:191–202.*

Galaburda, A. M. (1983). Developmental dyslexia: Current anatomical research. Proceedings of the 33rd annual conference of The Orton Dyslexia Society. *Annals of Dyslexia, 33,* 41–45.

Geschwind, N. (1984). The biology of dyslexia: The after-dinner speech. In D. B. Gray & J. F. Kavanaugh (Eds.), *Behavioral measures of dyslexia* (pp. 1–19). Parkton, MD: York.

Gilligan, J. (1996). *Violence: Reflections on a national epidemic.* New York: Vintage Books.

Green, C., & Chee, K. (1994). *Understanding ADD: Attention deficit disorder.* New York: Doubleday.

Hallowell, E. M., & Ratey, J. J. (1994a). *Driven to distraction.* New York: Pantheon.

Hallowell, E. M., & Ratey, J. J. (1994b). *Answers to distraction.* New York: Pantheon.

Hammill, D. D., & Bryant, B. R. (1998). *The learning disabilities inventory.* Austin, TX: PRO-ED.

Hooker, K. (1992). Possible selves and perceived health in older adults and college students. *Journal of Gerontology: Psychological Sciences,* 47:85–95.

Ingersoll, B. D., & Goldstein, S. (1993). *Attention deficit disorder and learning disabilities: Realities, myths and controversial treatments.* New York: Doubleday.

Irlen, H. (1991). *Reading by the colors: Overcoming dyslexia and other learning disabilities through the Irlen method.* Garden City, NY: Avery.

James, W. (1890). *The principles of psychology.* New York: Henry Holt.

Jamison, K. R. (1995). *An unquiet mind.* New York: Random House.

Johnson, D. J., & Myklebust, H. R. (1971). *Learning disabilities.* New York: Grune & Stratton.

Jordan, D. R. (1989a). *Overcoming dyslexia in children, adolescents, and adults* (1st ed.). Austin, TX: PRO-ED.

Jordan, D. R. (1989b). *Jordan prescriptive/tutorial reading program for moderate and severe dyslexia.* Austin, TX: PRO-ED.

Jordan, D. R. (1996a). *Overcoming dyslexia in children, adolescents, and adults* (2nd ed.). Austin, TX: PRO-ED.

Jordan, D. R. (1996b). *Teaching adults with learning disabilities.* Malabar, FL: Krieger.

Jordan, D. R. (1998). *Attention deficit disorder: ADHD and ADD syndromes,* (2nd ed.). Austin, TX: PRO-ED.

Jordan, D. R. (1999). *Jordan Dyslexia Assessment/Reading Program* Austin, TX: PRO-ED.

Kauffman, J. M., & Hallahan, D. P. (1996). *The illusion of full inclusion: A comprehensive critique of a current special education bandwagon.* Austin, TX: PRO-ED.

Kirk, S. A. (1962). *Educating exceptional children.* Boston: Houghton Mifflin.

Kogan, N. (1990). Personality and aging. In J. E. Birren & K. W. Shaie (Eds.), *Handbook of the psychology of aging* (3rd ed.) (pp. 330–346). New York, Academic Press.

Lee, A. T., & Cerami, A. (1990). Modifications of proteins and nucleic acids by reducing sugars: Possible role in aging. In E. L. Schneider & J. W. Rowe (Eds.), *Handbook of the biology of aging* (3rd. ed.) (pp. 116–130). New York: Academic Press.

Lehmkuhle, S., Garzia, R. P., Turner, L., Hash, T., & Baro, J. A. (1993). A defective visual pathway in children with reading disability. *New England Journal of Medicine, 328,* 989–996.

Lichtheim, L. (1885). On aphasie. *Brain, 7,* 432–484.

Livingstone, M. S., Rosen, G. D., Drislane, F. W., & Galaburda, A. M. (1991). Physiological and anatomical evidence for a magnicellular deficit in developmental dyslexia. *Proceedings of the National Academy of Sciences, USA, 88,* 7943–7947.

Llinas, R. (1993). Coherent 40-Hz oscillation characterizes dream state in humans. *Proceedings of the National Academy of Sciences, 90,* 2078–2081.

Naglieri, J. A., & Reardon, S. M. (1993). Traditional IQ is irrelevant to learning disabilities—intelligence is not. *Journal of Learning Disabilities, 26*(2), 127–133.

Orton, S. T. (1925). "Word-blindness" in children. *Archives of Neurology and Psychiatry, 14,* 581–615.

Osman, B. B., & Blinder, H. (1982). *Nobody to play with: The social side of learning disabilities.* New York: Random House Publishers.

Park, D. C. (1992). Applied cognitive aging research. In F. I. M. Craik & T. A. Salthouse (Eds.), *The handbook of aging and cognition* (pp. 449–493). Hillsdale, NJ: Lawrence Erlbaum Associates.

Pennington, B. F. (1991). *Diagnosing learning disorders: A neuropsychological framework.* New York: Guilford.

Ramachandran, V. S. (1993). Behavioral and magnetoencephalographic correlates of plasticity in the adult human brain. *Proceedings of the National Academy of Science, USA, 90,* 10413–10420.

Raskin, M. A., & Peskind, E. R. (1992). Alzheimer's disease and other dementing disorders. In J. E. Birren, R. B. Sloane, & G. D. Cohen (Eds.), *Handbook of mental health and aging* (2nd ed.) (pp. 478–513). New York: Academic Press.

Ratey, J. J., & Johnson, C. (1997). *Shadow syndromes.* New York: Pantheon.

Recer, P. (1998, November 24). Test detects attention deficit disorder. *Tulsa World,* (p. A6). Tulsa, OK.

Reiff, H. B., Gerber, P. J., & Ginsberg, R. (1993). Definitions of learning disabilities from adults with learning disabilities: The insider's perspective. *Learning Disability Quarterly, 16,* 114–125.

RSA. (1985). *Program policy directive.* Washington, DC: U.S. Office of Special Education and Rehabilitation Services.

Salthouse, T. A. (1991a). Cognitive facets of aging well. *Generations, 15*(1), 35–38.

Salthouse, T. A. (1991b). Mediation of adult age differences in cognition by reductions in working memory and speed of processing. *Psychological Science, 2*(3), 179–183.

Schacter, D. L. (1996). *Searching for memory.* New York: Basic Books.

Shapiro, F. (1995). *Eye movement desensitization and reprocessing: Basic principles, protocols, and procedures.* New York: Guilford.

Shaywitz, S. (1996, November). Dyslexia: A new model. *Scientific American* (pp. 2–8).

Schieber, F. (1992). Aging and the senses. In J. E. Birren, K. W. Sloane, & G. D. Cohen (Eds.), *Handbook of mental health and aging* (2nd ed.) (pp. 252–306). San Diego, CA: Academic Press, Inc.

Silver, L. (1985, November). *The learning disabled adult: Who is he? What is he?* Symposium conducted by the Menninger Foundation, Topeka, KS.

Slingerland, B. (1976). *The Slingerland screening tests for identifying children with specific language disabilities.* Cambridge, MA: Educators Publishing Service, Inc.

Spirduso, W. W., & MacRae, P. G. (1990). Motor performance and aging. In J. E. Birren & K. W. Schaie (Eds.), *Handbook of the psychology of aging* (3rd. ed.) (pp. 183–200). New York: Academic Press.

Stanovich, K. D. (1993). Dysrationalia: A new specific learning disability. *Journal of Learning Disabilities, 26* (8), 501–515.

Still, G. F. (1902). Some abnormal psychical conditions in children. *Lancet, i,* 1008–1012, 1077–1082, 1163–1168.

Tallal, P., Miller, S., & Fitch, R. (1993). Neurobiological basis of speech: A case for the preeminence of temporal processing. *Annals of New York Academy of Sciences, 682*(6), 74–81.

Tranel, D., Hall, L. E., Olson, S., & Tranel, N. N. (1987). Evidence for a right-hemisphere developmental learning disability. *Developmental Neuropsychology, 3,* 113–127.

Travis, J. (1996, February 17). Let the games begin. *Science News, 149,* 104–106.

Tredgold, A. F. (1908). *Mental deficiency (amentia).* New York: W. Wood.

Voeller, K. K. S. (1986). Right-hemisphere deficit syndrome in children. *American Journal of Psychiatry, 143,* 1004–1009.

Voeller, K. K. S. (1991). Social-emotional learning disabilities. *Psychiatric Annals* 21:735–41.

Wacker, J. (1975). *The dyslogic syndrome.* Dallas: Texas Association for Children with Learning Disabilities.

Warren, P., & Capehart, J. (1995). *You & your A.D.D. child: How to understand and help kids with attention deficit disorder.* Nashville, TN: Thomas Nelson Publishers.

Wechsler, D. (1994). *Wechsler Adult Intelligence Scale-III.* San Antonio, TX: Psychological Corporation.

Weisel, L. P. (1992). *POWERPath to adult basic learning.* Columbus, OH: The TLP Group.

Weiss, G., & Hechtman, L. T. (1993). *Hyperactive children grown up* (2nd ed.). New York: Guilford.

Weiss, L. (1995). *ADD on the job: Making your ADD work for you.* Dallas, TX: Taylor Publishing Company.

Woodcock, R. W. (1991). *Woodcock-Johnson Psycho-Educational Battery, Revised.* Circle Pines, MN: American Guidance Service.

INDEX